A VINDICATION OF THE CHURCH OF SCOTLAND'S INDIA MISSIONS

Owing to the antiquity and rarity of this book, certain pages are regrettably absent, and readability is compromised due to the blurring of the original text. If you possess any insights regarding the availability of these missing sections, kindly inform us. Your assistance is crucial in ensuring the completion of this significant work for the benefit of future generations.

A

VINDICATION

OF THE

CHURCH OF SCOTLAND'S INDIA MISSIONS

BEING

THE SUBSTANCE OF AN ADDRESS

BEFORE THE GEN ASSEMBLY OF THE CHURCH

ALEXANDER DUFF

GYAN

Published by

Gyan Publishing House
5, Ansari Road
Daryaganj, New Delhi-110002
Phone: 011-47034999, 9811692060
E-mail: books@gyanbooks.com

Distribution Network
gyanbooks.com
India, USA, Canada, UK, Australia

ISBN: 978-93-6780-580-0 (HB)

First Published, 1837

2nd Impression 2024

Printed at: Gyan Press, Delhi.

A VINDICATION OF THE CHURCH OF SCOTLAND'S INDIA MISSIONS
Author: ALEXANDER DUFF

A VINDICATION

OF THE

CHURCH OF SCOTLAND'S INDIA MISSIONS:

BEING

THE SUBSTANCE OF AN ADDRESS,

DELIVERED

BEFORE THE GENERAL ASSEMBLY OF THE CHURCH,

ON WEDNESDAY, MAY 24, 1837.

BY THE

REV. ALEXANDER DUFF, D.D.,

THE ASSEMBLY'S FIRST MISSIONARY TO INDIA.

PUBLISHED AT THE SPECIAL REQUEST OF THE GENERAL ASSEMBLY.

Tenth Thousand.

EDINBURGH:

PRINTED AND PUBLISHED BY

JOHN JOHNSTONE, 2, HUNTER SQUARE,

AND SOLD BY J. NISBET AND CO., LONDON.

MDCCCXXXVII.

PREFACE.

I. The following Address, being published at the special request of the General Assembly, now appears as nearly as possible in the form in which it was originally delivered. Under two or three heads only, have a few additional sentences been inserted, in order to render the meaning less liable to misapprehension.

II. In the course of a single Address, on a subject so vast and all-comprehensive, it was not possible, ever and anon, to step aside, for the purpose of pointing out *all* the *exceptions* from a *general rule*—or *all* the *modifications*, real or conceivable, of a *general principle*. On this account, it was my original intention to append to the Address a series of annotations, partly illustrative and partly confirmatory. But the length, to which I now find the Address, when printed, has extended, seems to forbid the realization of this intention.

I must, therefore, throw myself on the candour and indulgence of the Christian reader. Conscious as I am of cherishing no desire, save that of promoting God's glory, by the conversion of lost souls:—and entertaining, as I do, a brotherly affection towards all that love the Lord Jesus in spirit and in truth:—I shall be rejoiced to receive the friendly remarks or suggestions of *any minister or member of any congregation of professing Christians* in this land, relative to any of the topics introduced into the present Address.

Any communication, directed to the care of the Publisher, will be sure to reach me.

III. People in this country, are ever apt to conceive of India, as if it were a mere Asiatic province of limited territorial extent, like some section of the Island of Great Britain. It is necessary, therefore, constantly to remind them that, in extent, India more resembles Europe than Britain:—and how much more than any mere section of the latter? Consequently, though the Brahmanical system, as elsewhere remarked, "may be said to preserve, through the wide extent of its baneful domination, a sort of universal identity in fundamental principles, yet in the practical development of these principles, it may exhibit modifications that are endlessly or even capriciously diversified. So that what may be strictly and literally true of the mental habitudes, the social and religious practices, of the people of one city or province, may require some qualification when predicated of the inhabitants of another." From overlooking this essential circumstance, the statements of Missionaries situated in different parts of India, have sometimes been pronounced, erroneous, exaggerated, distorted, or, even contradictory. Whereas the truth may be, that each may all the while be conveying a scrupulously exact Report of his own individual findings, and local experience.

Would it be reasonable, for instance, on the part of a Hindu, to call in question the accuracy of any part of an account of the state of Christianity and Christian society in Edinburgh :—on the ground of its differing considerably from the report given to him by one man from Copenhagen; another, from Lisbon; and another, from Cape Matapan, in Greece? And yet, this, *in principle*, is but the counterpart of the mode in which a native of Britain is sometimes led to set aside, the *apparently* conflicting reports of individuals, that happen to have been located, in different and distant parts of the widely scattered provinces of India.

Besides, it ought to be borne in mind, that *different* individuals may see *the same objects* with *different eyes*. From this cause also, the reports of different observers may considerably vary, and yet one and all of them may be honest, conscientious men.

Look, for instance, at the reports of different individuals relative to the practical difficulties to be encountered in attempting to evangelize such a country as India.. While some have represented them as *absolutely insuperable*, have not others been disposed to run into the opposite extreme of *unduly lessening* their real magnitude? And yet who can doubt that the advocates of both extremes have often been honourable men, though both must be allowed to be equally wide of the truth?

If one man, from a certain peculiarity of mind, may see things, as through a telescope, unduly magnified; while another man, from some other peculiarity of mind, may see the same things, as through an inverted telescope, unduly diminished :—will not the report of the latter be as unaccordant with the reality as that of the former?

To imagine a mole-hill to be a mountain is no doubt a great mistake. But to imagine a mountain to be merely a mole-hill is surely a mistake equally great. To see things less than the reality seems just as deceptive as to see them larger than the reality.

Difficulties unduly magnified may scare the timorous, but will never daunt the courage of the brave. Difficulties, unduly diminished, may allure the timid and leave them floundering amid unexpected shoals and quicksands—while the brave may be deceived by the appearance of imaginary triumphs.

The grand thing is, as in all other cases, to endeavour to avoid either extreme. On a subject of this nature, however, no two men can scarcely be found so similarly circumstanced, in respect to mental powers, habits of reflection, and opportunities of observation, as to form precisely the same estimate. It is not possible, therefore, to fix any standard to which *all* opinions can be brought for admeasurement.

IV. It did not fall in with the object of the following address specially to advert to the important cause of female education in the Presidency of Bengal. The author, however, may here be permitted to transcribe a few brief notices, written some time ago, at the request of a friend, and published in the Appendix to an admirable sermon of the Hon. and Rev. Baptist Noel, preached in behalf of the Society in London for promoting Female Education in China, India, and the East.

1. While the education of males, more or less diverse in character and limited in extent, prevails pretty generally among the better classes throughout Eastern India, the education of females, from the operation of various causes, is not only almost universally neglected, but neglected designedly and systematically, as in itself not less mean and disreputable, than repugnant to the immemorial usages, social and religious, of the people.

2. In such an unpropitious state of things, immediate, rapid, wide-spread success in any scheme of female education, however skilfully devised, or vigorously prosecuted, is not to be anticipated. From the unnatural constitution of Hindu society, the education of females, in a national point of view, cannot possibly precede, cannot even be contemporaneous with the education of males. The education of the former, on any great national scale, must, from the very nature of their position, which those only who have been in India can at all adequately comprehend, follow in the wake of the enlightened education of the latter. In a word, a generation of educated males, *i. e.*, educated after the European model, must be the precursor of a generation of educated females.

3. Must we then, it may be asked, in the meanwhile sit still, and desist from the attempt to achieve *anything* in the department of female education? No, by no means. Though great things cannot, at this moment, be undertaken, still something may be done, and we are never to "despise the day of small things."

Already have British example, British intercourse, and British philanthropy, partially broken down in many places, the three thousand years' accumulated force of native prejudice; and female schools, for *elementary* education, have, in consequence, sprung up in different and distant parts of India. Mrs Wilson of Calcutta has, in this respect, done all that devoted piety and superior ability could have attempted; or rather, all that the adverse state of hereditary native feeling could have brooked. Her day-school has, for some years past, been attended by upwards of 200 female children, chiefly, however, of the lower and poorer *castes*. But, from *the immaturity of their mind, the contracted period of their attendance, and the all but impossibility of tracing them after their removal from school, and re-immersion into all the abominations of the vilest idolatry* "beneath the circuit of the sun," little, very little, in the way of permanent beneficial result can, in the present state of things, be expected to result from the operations of such a seminary.

The Orphan School, on the other hand, (though necessarily very limited in its range,) on account of the entire separation of the children from the votaries of heathenism, and the prolonged period of their attendance, promises to be productive of the happiest permanent effects.

4. After all, the great hope of female education in India, must arise from the present decidedly cheering prospects of male education.

Every genuine native Christian must, as a matter of course, be desirous of training up his children, male and female, in the "nurture and admonition of the Lord;" and though the number of this description in Eastern India is as yet exceedingly scanty, there is every reason to hope that, through the Divine blessing, fresh accessions will be yearly made to it.

But, apart altogether from the consideration of the growing class of native Christians, there is another and far more rapidly increasing one, that must annually swell the aggregate of those friendly to female improvement; I allude to the multiform class that aims at the acquisition of European literature and science, through the medium of the English language. From various concurrent causes, which it is needless for me here to detail, thousands of native youth have now begun to flock to Government and Missionary Institutions, there to enter on the career of English education; and, if the future keep pace proportionately with the past, these thousands will ere long be multiplied ten-fold, and ultimately a hundred-fold.

Now, it may safely be laid down as an undoubted axiom, that every individual who receives a thorough English education, whether he become a convert to Christianity or not, will, with it, imbibe much of the English spirit,—*i. e.*, become intellectually Anglicised; and hence, will inevitably enrol himself in the catalogue of those who assert the right of females to be emancipated from the bondage of ignorance. This is not a legitimate inference only, it is a statement of the results of past experience.

As an illustration of this remark, I may here state, that, about six years ago, I happened to be present at a debating society, composed of forty or fifty young men, who had acquired, or were then acquiring, an English education at the Government Hindu College. The subject of debate was,—"Whether females ought to be educated?"

Several of the senior members spoke with great fluency, and *all*, without one exception, pled the propriety of female instruction. One young man, with almost heroic fearlessness, asked, "Is it alleged by any that female education is prohibited, if not by the letter, at least by the spirit of some of our Shasters? if so, and if any of the Shasters be really found to advance any thing so contrary to reason, I, for one, will trample them under my feet." And this declaration was rapturously hailed by the plaudits of his associates.

Another, a youth of about fourteen or fifteen, towards the end of the discussion, rose up, remarking, that he had "listened with great delight to the arguments of the other gentlemen, but that one had escaped them, which he would now beg leave to advance. He would prove, by *geometry*, that females ought to be educated." All were instantly on the tiptoe of expectation, to hear what this geometrical argument might prove. It turned out to be a somewhat vague and fanciful application of one of the axioms of Euclid, and hence designated a geometrical argument. The occasion, however, and the time, and the place,—the speaker's caste and garb, and youthful countenance, beaming with dawning intelligence,—the dreary retrospect of ages of ancestorial female degradation, and the budding prospects of futurity,—all, all tended to invest the argument with an ominous significance that does not inherently belong to it. It was, in substance, as follows:—

"Is it conceded that *men* ought to be educated? Undoubtedly it is. And why is the concession made in their favour? Why not as well educate these cocoa trees? (pointing to those around the house.) Oh, we are told the reason is, that men have got souls, or minds, and these trees have not. And why is it that men's having souls should lead to their being educated? Because these souls are found, from experience, to be susceptible of growth, and, consequently, of cultivation; and, if susceptible of cultivation, ought they not to be cultivated? Assuredly they ought, else they must be waste and useless, and not fulfilling the design of their being. It is allowed, then, on all hands, that men's souls or minds ought to be cultivated—in other words, that men ought to be educated.

"Well, and have not females got souls or minds? Many of our Mussulman countrymen think not. But our Pandits, (learned men,) in all their folly, have never appealed to the Shasters for any such absurdity as this. So, then, it is quite orthodox for us to believe and assert that females have got souls—and if so, these must, like the souls of men, be capable of growth, capable of being cultivated. And if, because men have got souls capable of cultivation, it is granted that these ought to be cultivated; when it is acknowledged that females have got souls capable of cultivation, ought these not to be cultivated too? Surely they ought; because, 'things that are equal to the same thing, are equal to one another.' Hence I conclude, that females ought to be educated."

It must not, however, be inferred, that all those who *in theory* thus advocate the cause of female education, are in circumstances to carry out the theory immediately into practice. Over the present generation, little or no control can be exercised by the greater part of them. But, as time rolls on, they become the heads of families themselves, and then will they be prepared, in many instances at least, to give practical effect to their better judgment.

At the same time, it must be borne in mind, that views of selfish, worldly expediency in manhood, may interpose to arrest the flowing current of many a generous determination in youth. But as the number augments, a new society will be gradually forming, that will eventually burst through all the fetters of a degrading, domineering, superstition. In the intermediate transition state, the cause of female enlightenment will be espoused, *in theory*, by a constantly increasing number; and by another increasing, though smaller number, it will be realised *in practice* too; till the halcyon period arrives, when universal theory shall run parallel with universal practice.

God grant that the period may be hastened, and that a richer effusion of his grace may descend on all who prize the privilege of being fellow-workers with him, in bringing in the everlasting kingdom.

V. In the following Address, the votaries of the Brahmanical superstition are chiefly referred to,—because these constitute the vast majority of the people of Hindustan. It must not, however, be forgotten, that there is a very large Mahammadan population—of many millions—interspersed throughout all the provinces. The proportion of Hindus and Mahammadans varies exceedingly in different districts;—the latter being, in some places, in the ratio of a tenth, or a twentieth, or even less—and in others, greatly preponderant in numbers over the former. On this subject, Mr Adam, lately employed by Government as a commissioner to ascertain the state of native education, has furnished some very original and interesting details.

And, besides both these classes, there are numerous aboriginal tribes thinly scattered over the almost impenetrable forests of the interior, and the almost inaccessable mountain ranges on the frontiers, that have never acknowledged the supremacy of Brahma, or bowed beneath the sword of the false Prophet. Numerically, however, these tribes constitute but an atom of the dense mass of the population of Hindustan.

VI. It will be observed also, that the *original* station of Calcutta is chiefly referred to in the subsequent pages. When the former statement appeared, this happened to be the only Missionary station then occupied by the General Assembly of our Church. And in vindicating that statement from certain *misconceptions* that had arisen respecting some of its parts, I was compelled, by the nature of the case, to refer, in a great measure, to that scene of action, of which it professed to furnish a specific account.

With what zeal, and ability, and judgment, and prayerfulness, the Calcutta Mission has been carried on for the last two or three years, under the unwearied superintendence of Mr Mackay, and Mr Ewart, has abundantly appeared from the reports of the Committee. May the Lord reward them by the richest effusions of his Holy Spirit on their labours of love! Ere long their hands will be strengthened by the addition of a fellow-labourer of congenial spirit. Mr M'Donald,—who has, in the style of primitive devotedness, relinquished a pastoral charge in the land of his fathers, for the sake of enjoying the honour and the privilege of "preaching the unsearchable riches of Christ to the Gentiles,"—will in a few months set sail for Calcutta.

In order to obviate any misapprehension which may possibly have arisen, from any cause, in the mind of any individual, at home or abroad, I must here put on record the delightful circumstance,—viz., that, among the Assembly's Missionaries in Calcutta, not only has the most perfect unanimity prevailed as to the grand general principles on which the Mission has hitherto been conducted, but also the most perfect unanimity as to the minutest details connected with the practical development of these principles. And, in this perfect unanimity, the Missionaries in Calcutta have partaken merely in common with the Assembly's acting Committee in Edinburgh.

Under Mr Anderson, the Madras station promises to become a fruitful vineyard.

Of the varied and indefatigable labours of Dr Wilson at Bombay, and Mr Mitchell at Poonah, it is impossible to speak, without the warmest feelings of gratitude towards God. May He be pleased in mercy, long to spare such labourers to be a blessing to the millions of Western India! From Calcutta, on the East; Madras, on the South; and Bombay, on the West;—may such branches of the "vine of the Lord's own planting," shoot forth, as shall one day unite, and interweave their foliage over the plains of central Hindustan!

VII. One important subject not even alluded to, in what follows, is that of providing *suitable accommodation* for carrying on the different departments of Missionary operation in Calcutta. From a statement drawn up by the author about two years ago, he begs to submit to the reader the following quotation:—

"At present there is no adequate accommodation provided for the use of the Mission in Calcutta. If Lectures are to be delivered on Christian Evidence and Doctrine, &c., there is no Lecture-room; neither is there any room for School Library, School-book Depository, Apparatus, &c. For these purposes the Missionaries have hitherto been obliged to devote a part of their own dwelling-houses. For the use of the Institution, as at present conducted, a large native house has been hired, every corner of which is more than occupied. But, though it is the best that could be had, the situation has been found decidedly unhealthy, and the apartments, from their small size, excessively incommodious. Partly from the situation of the house, and partly from the small size of the rooms, these at times become heated to a degree that is dreadfully oppressive to the pupils, and altogether killing to the teachers. During the height of the hot season the thermometer has been found to rise daily to 105 and 106 degrees, and that too in a half-tainted atmosphere: whereas, in a larger and more airy building, the temperature might be reduced several degrees, and that in a purer atmosphere. Besides, the great number and the scattered position of the present apartments render twofold greater the labour and exhaustion of vigilant superintendence than would otherwise be necessary.

"Need the Committee say more? To avoid the hazard and expense of a failure, neither they nor the Missionaries did at the outset ask for buildings of any description. They chose rather to survey the field, and ascertain its capabilities. This having been done, the experiment of cultivating it was immediately tried. And as the result of nearly five years of prayerful labour and patient waiting upon their God, they have now with grateful hearts to report, that through the favour of Him from whom all blessings flow, the experiment has succeeded beyond all expectation. During this period God has been pleased in an especial manner to further their designs for the emancipation of the Hindu mind. Being able, therefore, with gratitude to God, to point to a triumphant success,—to several conversions,—to numbers of educated natives that are ready to attend lectures and discourses on the Christian Faith,—to *six hundred* youths under literary, scientific, and religious instruction, many of whom promise fair to exercise a prodigious influence on the destinies of India,—and to *hundreds more*, who have been *actually pressing* for admission, and *actually excluded, for want of space to hold them*,—they simply crave for the means of providing plain but suitable accommodation in the form of Class-rooms, Lecture-rooms, &c., in order to enable them more vigorously to prosecute operations so happily begun, and so exuberant with the prospect of glorious results. Will the people of Scotland, then, refuse the necessary means? The Committee cannot persuade themselves that in such circumstances a refusal is possible. They propose accordingly, to open a separate special subscription, to be designated "The Building Fund." And they urgently recommend the subject to the favourable attention of the friends of Missions generally, and the members of the Church of Scotland in particular.

"It is calculated that the purchase of ground and the erection of buildings of the plainest possible description, and yet sufficiently ample for carrying on the preparatory and higher courses of instruction on so very large and extended a scale, cannot, in a place like Calcutta, cost much less than five or six thousand pounds. Still, considering the real magnitude of the object to be accomplished, it is presumed it would be difficult to name a more profitable outlet for the benevolence of those, who long and pray for the establishment of Messiah's kingdom over the hideous and gigantic systems of Pantheism and Idolatry in Hindustan."

VIII. Another special object may here be introduced to the notice of the Christian public of this land.

The great hope of India's amelioration, consists in the success of the attempt to raise up a race of duly qualified native labourers—

who shall become teachers and preachers of the everlasting Gospel to their own benighted countrymen. In order effectually to accomplish this great end, those who enter a Christian Institution, like that of the General Assembly, as boys, must remain there till they attain to years of maturity. But how is such an extension of the period of attendance to be secured? Sometimes, the parents or friends are both able and willing to support a young man, during the whole course of his instruction, however prolonged. But it not unfrequently happens, that, in the case of young men of *the greatest promise*, parents, from poverty, are unable,—or, from different causes, unwilling, after a very limited time, to supply the necessary support. What then is to be done in cases of this description? Are young men of talent and ingenuous disposition, who long with the most intense anxiety, to treasure up all the stores of our knowledge, human and divine, that they may become "burning and shining lights" in the midst of a "darkness that may be felt;"—are such young men to be frustrated in their hopes, and, after two or three years of promise, to be tossed back again into the "horrible pit and miry clay" of idolatry and superstition? Surely this is a disastrous issue which the Christian people of this land would labour to prevent, if they could. But it is in the power of thousands to prevent it, if they will.

All that is required is, that the Missionaries, who superintend the Central Institution, should have at their disposal, a number of permanent scholarships, of from five, to ten, or twelve pounds a-year. The prospect of such a scholarship, as a reward after a few year's diligent attendance in the Institution, would operate as a stimulus on many a talented and promising young man,—by holding out to him the assured hope of being able to prosecute his studies to a completion—and of thus becoming qualified, through the blessing of God, to act as a mighty instrument in arousing thousands from the slumber of ages.

Sums of from £250, to £500, would found, *in perpetuity*, scholarships of different grades—and thus prove the means, under God, of securing a *succession* of highly enlightened men, that might otherwise be entirely lost to themselves and to their country.

Already have two philanthropic ladies, whose names I am not as yet privileged to announce, resolved to devote the munificent sum of *one thousand pounds* to the purpose of establishing two or more such scholarships. May their noble example be speedily followed by others, who may thus raise to themselves, in the onward lapse of ages, a series of living monuments, more lasting and precious far, than the loftiest piles of "marble or of brass!"

XI. There is one other subject to which, in conclusion, I would crave the earnest attention of the Christian people of this land.

Has not our Lord and Saviour left us a *model* of prayer? And is it not a memorable circumstance that, out of the *six* petitions which constitute that prayer, there are *two*, and these the *first in order*, specially devoted to that great cause which led him to endure "the agony and bloody sweat?" How comes it, then, that ministers, in the public services of the sanctuary; and private Christians in their closet and family devotional exercises, *so often confine* all reference to the extension of the Redeemer's kingdom, *to one or two brief formal sentences at the conclusion of their prayers—and so often omit a specific reference to the subject altogether?*

Surely, this is not as it *ought to be.* Let us hope that the time is not far distant when no minister in the pulpit, and no member of a congregation in the closet, or at the family altar, shall ever forget in solemn earnestness to offer up the petition recommended and enforced by the divine Redeemer himself:—"Thy kingdom come: thy will be done on earth as it is done in heaven." And if the heaven-ordained practice of praying for the speedy diffusion of Gospel light throughout the world were to become regular and universal, would it not ultimately incite thousands to corresponding efforts, in order to realise the glorious object habitually prayed for? And would not *the general union of prayer and effort,* in extending the conquests of the cross and bringing in the everlasting kingdom, cause the windows of heaven to be opened, and the streams of grace to descend, like rain upon the new mown grass, or showers that water the spring?

EDINBURGH, *7th June* 1837.

VINDICATION

OF THE

CHURCH OF SCOTLAND'S INDIAN MISSIONS, &c.

MODERATOR,

WHEN, for the first time in my life, I had the honour of addressing this Venerable House, my task was chiefly expository. And when now, in all human probability, for the last time in my life, the same privilege is conferred, my task will be found chiefly vindicatory.

To the exposition given on the former occasion of the principles on which the original Mission of the Church of Scotland had been conducted in Calcutta, this House was pleased to affix the high stamp of its approbation. And is it too much to say, after the fertile experience of the last two years, that to the verdict and appeal of this House, the intelligence of the people of Scotland has most approvingly responded?

Owing to the multiplied opportunities already presented to me, in different parts of the country, for expounding at large the present state and contemplated objects of the Mission, it is wholly unnecessary on the present occasion to enter into minute details. But it were worse than forgetful, did I not thus publicly declare, that these favourable opportunities were nowhere limited by any unwillingness on the part of Ministers and members of this Church, either in their Presbyterial or individual capacity—were nowhere limited, save by the physical incapacities of the visiting agent. Farther, it were worse than ungrateful, did I not as publicly declare, that all these opportunities were signalised throughout by personal acts of kindness on the part of Ministers and members of this Church—acts of kindness so varied and undeserved—that I shall never find an adequate expression for them, save in the breathings of a grateful heart at a throne of grace. And, last of all, it were worse than obtuseness—it were moral blindness—did I not observe that these opportunities were not only opened up everywhere with amazing facility, but everywhere called forth such manifestations of what may be reckoned latent piety, and hitherto unthought of benevolence, as to prove, beyond all debate, that this Church is yet fraught with prodigious rallying powers—that it is no longer a dream or a vision on the part of her devoted friends, that by the breath of the Almighty's presence, she is yet to arise in renovated beauty,—and that, like the mighty Nazarite, snapping the bands designed to dwarf her stature and paralyse her power,—converting apparent weaknesses into enduring monuments of unequalled strength,—she is yet destined to stand forth before an awakened world, more pure, more stately, more majestic, more indomitable than ever.

To return to my own more immediate theme.—It may be known to many members of this House, that, while the exposition formerly submitted to it has been cordially approved of by many of the wisest and most enlightened Christian minds in the land, various objections have arisen in different quarters to some of its statements. But is there aught strange in this? What great cause has ever been advanced in the world, without calling forth a host of antagonisms? In the present case, however, the alleged objections are scarcely entitled to the name—since they are, every one of them, *misconceptions*, and *not* reasonable objections at all. I might, therefore, at once summarily dismiss them—prepared as I am to demonstrate, if need be, that they are all based either on palpable *misapprehensions* of some of my facts, or palpable *misinterpretations* of some portions of my language. Indeed, such is my own impression of their utter groundlessness, that my conviction is unalterable, that the greater part, if not all, of them, ought to be allowed to pass by unheeded and unnoticed—dancing their little hour, like bubbles, on the stream of great principles—and then evanish—leaving the stream to flow on, unaffected by their presence!

And if now I proceed rapidly to notice a few of the more prominent ones, it will be, not so much to refute what scarcely needs any refutation, as to employ these as so many occasions for fastening more deeply than ever, certain leading fundamental principles in the minds of all, and more particularly of the people of Scotland.

And since this House, under God, ought ever to be one of the great fountain-heads of unchanging principle in the delegated administration of the Christian economy on earth;—and since, besides, the eyes not only of the British Churches, but of the Protestant Churches throughout the world are at this moment intensely directed towards its proceedings;—it is a matter of mightiest import that the announcement of great principles, involved in the successful prosecution of the missionary enterprize, should go forth attested by the seal of its approbation and authority.

I. First of all, it is with extreme regret I have heard it alleged that the missionary labours of other churches and societies have been disparaged, or unduly undervalued in my former statement.

But what is the ground of this allegation? It is entirely of a negative character. It consists simply and solely in *the omission* of a formal specific reference to such labours. Now, I at once acknowledge that there may be cases where an omission may be tantamount to a disparagement. But I did not think before, neither am I persuaded now, that the case in question was one of these. How stands the matter? The General Assembly of this Church select and send forth an accredited agent, on a special mission to India. After a few years, this agent, in consequence of an afflictive visitation of Providence, over which he had no control, is necessitated to return, for a season, to his native land. What, in such circumstances, let me ask,—what more natural, than for this Assembly to call upon him to render an account of his stewardship? What more natural than to summon him, to lay before them a specific statement of the manner in which he had endeavoured to carry into execution that commission, with which they had been pleased to intrust him? This, accordingly, was what actually took place. And when the task assigned to me was so very distinct and clearly defined, would it not have been wholly irrelevant to have digressed into special notices of the missionary proceedings of *other* churches and societies? It was, therefore, the marked *peculiarity* of the object proposed to me, and *that alone*, which led to the *omission* in question.

Far from wishing, directly or indirectly, slightingly to overlook the missionary efforts of other denominations of Christians, God is my witness, that I have heretofore greatly rejoiced in these efforts,—and that, in common with my brethren, I have, both in public and in private, offered up fervent prayer and supplications to Almighty God for their increasing prosperity. Often have I gloried in the blessed fruit which they have already been privileged to reap in many a dry and parched land. And may I not add, that there is not a single member of this great Assembly that is not ready, in deep sincerity of soul, to ascribe praise and glory to God the Father, for all the real success which may have attended the labours of any Christian church or society in extending the Redeemer's kingdom over the world?

II. It has also been alleged that, in my former statement, I expressed myself with disrespect towards my predecessors and fellow-labourers in the missionary field.

Never, certainly, was any allegation more unfounded. The rare endowments, original and acquired, of many of the missionary body, both living and dead, and the unrivalled services which they have rendered, at once to the cause of Christianity and of Literature, have now become matters of history, and are far beyond my feeble unworthy praise. Of such men, accordingly, have I often spoken in terms of unbounded admiration. And, whatever my own private opinion may be, as to the intellectual and literary qualifications of many who have gone forth to the missionary field, I would hereby challenge the thousands and the tens of thousands who have now heard me address them in public, both in Scotland and in England, to refer, if they can, to a single instance wherein I have disrespectfully alluded to any one of them. On the contrary, I would again appeal, with equal confidence, to thousands and tens of thousands in this land, whether I have not often volunteered to dilate, in glowing terms, on the zeal, and devotedness, and sterling moral worth, of all of every denomination, with whom I happened to be familiarly acquainted, in and around the metropolis of British India?

On what, then, it may well be asked, can the charge of disparagement be possibly founded?—Solely on a singular misunderstanding of a passage in the original statement, to this effect:—"While the office of the Missionary is held up as the highest walk of Christian philanthropy, it must still be asked, How comes it that our great men, our giants in theology, have left it to be occupied by babes and striplings?"

Who may not perceive, at half a glance, the totally opposite bearing and meaning of these words, when viewed in connection with the context, from what the charge of disparagement seems to imply?

Often, in the course of my numerous journeyings at home, have I been accosted, by men of note, somewhat after this manner:—"Oh, the office of a Missionary is, beyond all question, the highest, noblest, and most honourable in the Church of Christ,—it is the very office of the Apostles themselves! I wonder much at the scarcity of duly qualified labourers. Are there none of our students of divinity, none of our unprovided preachers of the Gospel, coming forward as candidates?" Wearied by such frequent protestations of supreme regard for an office in theory, while yet in practice it is in general so lightly esteemed, I have sometimes been constrained abruptly to respond:—"Oh, if you really do reckon the office of a Missionary to be so very high, and noble, and honourable, above all others, why don't you set the example, by becoming a candidate for it yourself? Rest assured, that *one such decisive act*, in proof of the sincerity of profession, would far more essentially benefit the great cause of missions, than hundreds of your eloquent sermons in the pulpit, and thousands of your flaming speeches on the platform!"

Now, it was entirely in reference to the apparent inconsistency, between the professions and the practice of such men, that that sentence was uttered, which has been so strangely misconstrued into the language of disrespect towards the missionary body. If any such disrespect had been at all intended, then, had the language in which it was conveyed a special directness of bearing towards myself. For, surrounded as I was at the moment of its utterance, by the Cookes' and the Mearns', the Burns' and the Gordons, and many more of the giant brood of our Scottish divines, I did, in deep and unfeigned humility, feel that, in *their* presence, I was nothing more, even after the toils and fatigues of a foreign service, than a very "babe and stripling" in theological experience and attainments.

And, after all, is it not a mere matter of fact, that, compared with those learned doctors, and other men of renown, who have their own, no doubt most satisfactory, reasons for remaining at home, they have, in general, been but "babes and striplings" that have hitherto been equipped and sent forth to the missionary warfare,—babes and striplings in intellectual and theological acquirements,—babes and striplings in experience of the functions of the ministerial office? Talk of Swartz, and Vanderkemp, and Morrison, and Ward, and Carey! Were not even these bright stars, in the missionary galaxy, comparatively dim and lustreless when they *first* arose in the horizon of heathen lands? And if, afterwards, they shone with a brilliancy that has since dazzled the Christian Church, how does that disprove the fact of the comparative obscurity of their earlier appearance in the missionary field?—how does that invalidate our view of the conduct of those veterans who, in their day and generation, preferred the downy repose and luxurious indulgences of home, to the dear-bought glory of death or victory, on the battle-field of an extending Christendom? Oh! until the day come, when that service, which holy apostles did surely account, beyond compare, the most god-like in which the heirs of glory can be engaged, shall attract to itself our most redoubted champions in the Christian warfare,—we have no more right to exult in the high nobility of our pedigree from the heroes of the Covenant, than the modern cowards of Missolonghi, or the crouching slaves of the Archipelago, to boast of their noble descent from the heroes of Marathon or Thermopylæ!

III. It has been alleged that, from my account of the *proverbial* subtilty of the Hindu mind, one would imagine that I considered the whole of the Hindu population to be transcendental philosophers.

Now, it so happens, in point of fact, that I actually asserted something the *direct contrary* of this. In express terms I stated, that these "transcendental philosophers" belonged exclusively to the *Brahmanical caste*. And in order to render, as I fondly imagined, all misconception utterly impossible, I remarked with emphasis, respecting "the mass of people," that "these were miserably ignorant, —as ignorant and brutish as the stocks and stones around them."

What, therefore, I *really* did state before, I now reiterate again, and will do so to the end of my life,—that, belonging to the *Brahmanical caste*, there *are learned men, distinguished for their logical and metaphysical subtilties*,—and that these, in number more or less, are everywhere found interspersed throughout the native community. In the north of Bengal there exists, what perhaps cannot be easily paralleled in all the world besides,—that is, a small town almost entirely consisting of clusters of schools, or colleges of Brahmans, exclusively engaged in the study of their own logical and metaphysical Shasters.

Now, what was the *practical inference* deduced from this undisputed and indisputable fact? It was this—that it would be *very desirable* for missionaries *in general*, and *absolutely necessary for, at least, some of them* to be prepared to successfully contend with this race of subtile dialecticians. What exact *proportion* these may bear to the general population, no one can tell;—and so far as the *practical inference* now stated is concerned, the determination of this point is a matter of comparatively little moment. The grand object to be kept in view is, that, almost everywhere, one or more of these metaphysicians by profession, are really to be met with—and that they are of the exalted order of Brahmans, before whom the mass of the people "bow down as before the gods—for limbs or fragments they are verily believed to be of the supreme Deity." Now, I appeal, whether, without the aid of the divine prerogatives of a Brahman, one metaphysical Hume has not effectually succeeded in convulsing the whole world of systematic Christian theologists?—and whether he has not supplied a file which, from our own Campbell down to our own Chalmers, has, for more than half a century, exercised some of the sharpest wits in Christendom? And, if this be so, in a case where neither credit nor reverence could have been enjoyed, beyond what simple intellect commanded, what may it not be in a country like India, where the metaphysician may claim for himself the reverence of a god, and challenge for his metaphysics an infallible authority?—After this, may I not again ask in triumph, whether some at least of the army of the faithful ought not to be specially panoplied, in order to encounter these subtile sons of

Brahma,—and cause their peculiar weapons to recoil on their own heads?.

IV. It has been alleged that some of my former statements went to prove, that all the millions of India must become good English scholars, before they can be expected to embrace the Christian faith.

This is one of those misapprehensions for which it is difficult to imagine even a plausible reason;—seeing that it is in *direct contradiction* to the express language formerly employed. But, without trespassing on the time of this House, with any recapitulation of what was then advanced, allow me at once to furnish an additional illustration of our design.

There are many here present who are thoroughly conversant with the past and present condition of the Highlands of Scotland. In their presence, then, I ask,—By what process have the Highlands been Christianized and civilized? Has it been by a violent attempt to extirpate the language of Ossian, that sang the tales of other years, with the view of substituting universally another and a better in its place? No: that were impossible;—since, violently to extirpate the language, would just be, violently to exterminate the people. Has it been by an exclusive attempt to transfuse into that language all the vast stores of modern knowledge? No: that, too, were impracticable. Copious to overflowing, the Gaelic must be allowed to be, in descriptive imagery;—and resistless as the mountain torrent, in its vocabulary of impassioned address. But let any man, who really understands the subject, conceive to himself the project of translating into Gaelic such a work as the "Encyclopædia Britannica," and he will soon be compelled to assent to the existence of the impracticability now referred to. What, then, was to be done? Precisely what sound judgment might suggest, and the necessity of the case seemed to demand. A middle course has been happily adopted and pursued. Are the people to be taught the elements of sound knowledge?—and is the Gospel to be preached to them in strains familiar and effective? Then, of necessity, must there be raised up a superior race of teachers and of preachers. And whence are these to be procured?—from a foreign land?—from among men, speaking a strange tongue? No: but *from among the people themselves.* And how, under the disadvantages now described, has this desirable object been accomplished? How have any of the natives of the Highlands been raised to pre-eminence in learning above their fellows? By an expedient the most natural and successful. The English language is, at present, the great storehouse of all knowledge. Well, this being so, what has been the conduct of Highland parents? It has been that of wisdom and sound understanding. They have just sent their children to English schools, to acquire the rudiments of useful knowledge. And all those, whose circumstances could afford it, have followed up this elementary instruction, by sending them to our English academies and English colleges. In this course, the sons of the north have no doubt to contend, more particularly at the outset, with vast difficulties, from which the sons of the south are wholly exempt,—and in the struggle to surmount which, the latter can manifest little sympathy. They have, in fact, to master an entirely foreign language; and cause to be transferred into it, those modes and habits of thought which, from earliest infancy, had been cast in a far different mould. On this subject I speak from painful experience, because the Gaelic is my mother tongue. But, agreeably to the proverb, diligence and perseverance will ever overcome all difficulties, not absolutely insuperable. Accordingly, is it not a simple statement of fact, that the sons of the north are everywhere found in our English schools, academies, and colleges, successfully grappling with the obstacles that impede their progress? Yea, are they not often found triumphantly bearing away the palm of superior scholarship from their southern compeers? And, after having enriched their own minds with the treasures of universal knowledge, in literature, science, and theology, through the medium of the English language, do we not find them return to their own romantic valleys and everlasting hills, richly laden with the stores which they have accumulated on a foreign territory?—Do we not find them vigorously and patriotically engage, in transmuting the more appropriate portions of these varied stores into materials, bearing the stamp and superscription of their own mother tongue? —Do we not find them in this way succeed, through the blessing of heaven, in diffusing the odours of sweetest incense, enkindled at the shrines of learning, or sanctified at the altars of piety, among the thousands and tens of thousands of an awakened, and gladdened, and edified people?

Now, this very process, which has been so eminently blessed to the Highlands of Scotland—this very process, which has converted these regions of thickest Popish darkness into a domain, enlightened by the cloudless rays of the Sun of Righteousness—this very process, which has transformed the Highlands, from being a mere hunting-field of "savage clans and roving barbarians," into a nursery of plants of renown that shall bloom and blossom in the climes of immortality;—this very process and none other, are we now labouring with all our might, through God's blessing, to apply to the regeneration of the universal mind of India.

While, therefore, as explained on a former occasion, it is confessed that "the *vernacular* languages alone are available for imparting *elementary* instruction to the *mass* of the people of Hindustan, it is insisted on as *a fact*, that these languages do not *at present* afford an *adequate medium* for communicating a knowledge of the *higher* departments of literature, science, and theology. Consequently, for the present, the *English* language must be viewed as the *medium of acquisition* to the thoroughly educated *few*; and the *vernacular* dialects to the ordinarily educated *many*. The *former* constitutes the channel of *contribution* to the reservoirs of those minds that are to be cultivated, so as to disseminate all knowledge; the *latter* will form the channels of *distribution* to those who must be satisfied with the mere elements of knowledge. The *former* unseals the inexhaustible fountain of all knowledge; the *latter* must serve as ducts to diffuse its vivifying waters over the wastes of a thirsty land. In a word, *the English language is the lever, which, as the grand instrument of conveying the entire range of knowledge, secular and sacred, seems destined, in the unfolding dispensations of Providence, to move all Hindustan!*"*

V. It has been strangely alleged that, from the representation formerly given, one would suppose that our scheme was, to *infidelize* the Hindus first, and Christianize them afterwards.

Without waiting to expose so very idle a misconception, I shall simply advance a few statements, calculated to rescue this important subject from that strange confusion of

* See former Exposition of the Church of Scotland's India Mission. Second Edition, p. 30, 31.

ideas which is so apt to gain currency among the unreflecting and unintelligent.

1*st*, My *first* statement is, that there is a yearly increasing demand for English education, more especially in the provinces of Gangetic India.

Of the truth of this statement, many indisputable proofs might be given. The Committee of Public Instruction, in their official report to Government, expressly declare, that "the study of English, to which many circumstances induce the natives to give the preference, and with it the knowledge of the learning of the West, is daily spreading." This, though of a general nature, is an authoritative testimony. But there is one practical test of the existing state and direction of the current of native feeling, in reference to education, which seems peculiarly decisive. There has been, for many years past, in Calcutta, a School-Book Society, partly supported by private contribution, and partly by the munificence of Government. The books of this society, remarks Mr Trevelyan, one of the Secretaries of Government, are sold to any body who chooses to purchase; and the proportions, in which they are disposed of, shew the relative demand that exists for the different kinds of learning. The statement of the sales which have been made during the last two years, extracted from the Society's recently published report, is as follows:—

English, ...	31,649	books.
Anglo-Asiatic, ...	4,525	,,
Bengali, ...	5,754	,,
Hindui, ...	4,171	,,
Hindustani, (or Urdu,) .	3,384	,,
Uriya, ...	834	,,
Persian, ...	1,454	,,
Arabic, ...	36	,,
Sanskrit, ...	16	,,

This enumeration is altogether *exclusive* of the many valuable English publications that constantly issue from the Serampore press; as well as of those sold at different private establishments in Calcutta. Can any proof appear more decisive of the growing taste of the natives for the English language? From the School-Book Society's Depository, there issue in the two learned languages of India only 52 works!—Arabic, 36; and Sanskrit, (believed to be the very language of the gods,) 16!—While, in the

English language, there is a sale of 31,649!—Who, after this, can pretend to doubt the accuracy of the averment respecting the rapidly increasing demand among the natives of Eastern India for the English language, and that improved literature and science of which it is the key?

2*d*, My *second* statement is, that the British Government in India not only encourages the native taste for English education, but also provides to a large extent the means of obtaining it.

When I last addressed this House, I specially adverted to Lord W. Bentinck's resolution to supersede the Persian, in the political department of the public service, and ultimately in every other, by the substitution of English. I adverted, at the same time, to several striking facts, illustrative of the effect of this resolution in stimulating numbers of the higher classes of natives to the study of the English language. Little did I know that, at the very time of my addressing this House, there was, midway on its passage from India to England, an edict which more than confirmed all that had ever been advanced on the subject—an edict that promises to constitute a new era in the history of India.

Up to the 7th March 1835, the great object of the Government schemes of education had been, to initiate the natives into a knowledge of their own literature, science, and religion, through the medium of their own learned languages. By the Government enactment* of that date, this object was totally changed. It was therein decreed by the Governor-General in Council, that "the great object of the British Government ought to be the promotion of European literature and science among the natives of India; and that all the funds appropriated for the purposes of education, would be best employed on *English* education alone."

This enactment has already been followed up with such rapid effect by the Committee of Public Instruction, that, within the last two years, the Government English Institutions in the Presidency of Bengal have been *more than doubled*. The number of purely Government Institutions is now *twenty-seven*; and the revenue for their support exceeds £25,000 per annum. All of these, except four

* See the nature and tendency of this enactment expounded at large in a pamphlet just published by the author, entitled, "New Era of the English Language and English Literature in India." Printed and published by J. Johnstone, Edinburgh; and sold by J. Nisbet, Berners Street, London.

Mahammadan and Sanskrit Colleges, are devoted to English education—and the funds, at present appropriated to these four, will gradually become available for the purposes of instruction in English literature and science.

Some of the first established of the English seminaries, such as the Hindu Colleges of Calcutta and Delhi, have already risen to the status of Collegiate Institutions. And all the rest have been carefully planted in large central towns, with the express design of raising them, by degrees, into Colleges, with a Principal, and Professors of English composition and literature, of mathematics and natural philosophy, &c., in each. From these central institutions, as from so many radiating points, it is also intended that branch-schools shall gradually emanate—so as ultimately to pervade, with elementary instruction, every district and village in the land.

As an exemplification at once of the growing demand for English, and of the liberal manner in which Government is prepared to meet it, I shall here refer to what took place about a *twelvemonth ago*, in the town of Hugli, about 30 miles north of Calcutta.

On the authority of the Government functionary, already named, I have to state that, when, last year, the new English seminary was opened in that town, English students flocked to it in such numbers, as to render the organization of them into classes a matter of difficulty,—and that there are now, about 1,400 native boys, learning *English only;* about 200, learning Arabic and Persian only; and upwards of a hundred, who are learning both English and Arabic or Persian. To this it is expressly added, that "notwithstanding this unprecedented concourse, the applications for English instruction are still extremely numerous; and there seems to be no limit to the number of scholars, except the number of masters whom the (Government) Education Committee is able to provide." In another place, the same competent authority positively declares, that, "in the numerous (English) seminaries under the Education Committee, there is no want of scholars—and that the difficulty is to provide masters enough to teach the numbers who are anxious to receive instruction."

3*d*, My *third* statement is, that, in order still farther to extend and perpetuate the thirst for English literature and science, the Government Committee in Calcutta have recently determined to provide the more advanced of their

English institutions with libraries of books in every department of knowledge.

This determination to provide the different institutions with libraries of English books is a truly noble one, and worthy of all commendation. In regard, however, to the *practical* execution of this grand design, a sense of duty compels me to make a few passing strictures. I had lately occasion, in another place, to refer to the same subject, and shall here simply repeat what was then advanced.

Had the libraries, ordered from England about a year ago, and now in all probability landed in Calcutta, "consisted of the choicest standard works in English literature and science,—so far all well. However much a Christian might regret the *absence* of all publications that unfold the ennobling doctrines and morals of Christianity, he would find some consolation in the circumstance that *true* literature and science had been substituted instead of a literature and science abounding with demonstrable *errors*. He would have to complain of an act of *omission*, and not of *commission*. But it is with pain and sorrow I have to observe, that while the libraries in question contain some of the very best books in the English language, they also contain some of the most useless, and some too of the very worst. There are, for the younger pupils, several excellent works:—but why ransack the dust-covered bookshop of some antiquated librarian for copies of *Cinderella, Puss in Boots, Jack the Giant-Killer, Tom Thumb, Little Red Riding Hood, the Devil on two Sticks*, &c.? Could this age of "the march of intellect" provide no better food for the newly-awakening minds of Hindu youth? But all these, you will say, are simply trash and trumpery:—that is all;—as they may be said to be comparatively harmless. Well, for adults, many most admirable works are provided. But there is a strange medley. If, for instance, under the general designation of "History and Biography," there are copies of *the Bible;* placed side by side are copies of Sale's translation of the *Koran*. If, under the head of "Poetry," there are copies of *Milton's* works, in 6 vols.; there are also copies of the entire works of *Byron*, in 17 vols. If, under the head of "Metaphysics and Moral Philosophy," there are copies of *Bacon's* Essays; there are also copies of *Hume's* Essays, in which the very foundations of Christianity are sapped and undermined. But why need I enumerate more? Enough has been advanced to entitle me to ask, Why this strange intermixture of light and darkness, truth and error? Why supply the newly emancipated intellects of Indian youth with poison simultaneously with wholesome food? As if India had not already enough of wild and fantastic absurdities in the speculations of its Pantheistic metaphysicians, or enough of prurient licentiousness in the revolting legends embodied in the Ramayan, and Maha Bharat, and other Sanskrit legends, that outrage decency and common sense;—why inundate, from the West, its rising institutions with the anti-Christian sophisms and crudities of Hume and Bentham, or the moral pestilence of Fielding and Byron? And why send forth all these productions, good, bad, and indifferent, in the name and by the authority of the British Governor-General of India—as if all were alike precious—and all alike bore the high stamp of his approbation?" *

4th, My *fourth* statement is, That a *thorough* English education, apart from religious instruction altogether, is entirely subversive of Hinduism.

The *rationale* of this I formerly explained at length, and shall not, on that account, again revert to it. The literature and science of the Hindus being incorporated with their religion, if you destroy the former, which abounds with palpable errors, by the introduction of the true literature and science of Europe, the foundations of the latter must be overthrown. Should this appear to any one, merely in the light of a plausible theory, let him ponder well the following unsuspicious testimonies from natives themselves, and say if they are not absolutely decisive of the question.

The once Brahman, but now Christian editor of the *Inquirer* newspaper, who himself received his English education at the Government Hindu College, where *no religion* is taught, thus strongly testifies:—"The Hindu College, under the patronage of Government, *has*, as indeed it *must* have, *destroyed many a native's belief in Hinduism*. How could a boy continue to worship the *sun*, when he understood that this luminary was not a *devatah*, (a divinity,) but a mass of inanimate matter? How could he believe in the injunctions of such Shasters as taught him lessons contrary to the principles inculcated by his lecturer in natural philosophy? The consequence was, that the

* See an Address, recently delivered in Exeter Hall, London, at the anniversary of the Church of Scotland's Foreign Missions.

castle of Hinduism was battered down. *No Missionary ever taught us* (meaning himself, the editor,) *to forsake the religion of our fathers; it was Government that did us this service.*"

Again, the native editor of the *Reformer*, another English newspaper, and the organ of the educated Hindus in Calcutta, contrasting the results of ordinary missionary labour with those realised by the Hindu College, thus emphatically asks:—"Has it (the college) not been the fountain of a new race of men amongst us? *Have all the efforts of the Missionaries given a tithe of that shock to the superstitions of the people which has been given by the Hindu College?* This at once shews that the means they pursue to overturn the ancient reign of Idolatry is not calculated to insure success, and ought to be abandoned for another which promises better success."

Whatever share prejudice, ignorance, or dislike, might have in leading the native editor to form so low an estimate of the fruit of *ordinary missionary exertion*, must not scepticism itself concede, that his testimony is conclusive as to the efficient power of a *thorough English education* in overturning the superstitions and idolatries of India?

5th, Here I might pause,—satisfied with having called the attention of the Christian public of this land to the all-important subjects now summarily detailed, at so early a stage of the progress of events, that shall one day terminate in a mighty crisis in the history of India,—but it may be well, briefly to sum up the four preceding statements.

There is now, more especially in Eastern India, a yearly increasing demand for English education; and there is a strong disposition, on the part of the British Government, to encourage this demand, as well as largely to provide the means of supplying it, by the establishing of numerous English institutions, and the founding of English libraries. But a thorough English education must, everywhere, prove destructive of the systems of Hinduism. Hence, as the Government schemes of education systematically exclude religion, the necessary effect of their operation must be, everywhere to subvert the idolatries and superstitions of the people, and then cast them adrift on the wide ocean of *infidelity*.

It is worse than idle to evade this conclusion, by merely pointing to the *present limited* results of such a system. Why are these results, at present, so limited? Simply because the sphere of operation of those plans, that inevitably lead to them, is as yet so contracted. And it is just because this sphere is as yet so circumscribed; it is just because the processes of change are as yet only coming into action, at the *commencement* of a *transition* state; it is just because, on that very account, it is, as yet, *quite possible*, through God's blessing, to overtake a movement that will be ever progressive in a sphere ever widening;—that I feel so intensely anxious to rouse and direct the attention of British Christians to the present extraordinary state of things in India.

The Hindu College of Calcutta, from having reached maturity, has already given a tremendous shock to the systems of Hinduism. And, as "like causes will, in similar circumstances, produce like effects," are we not constrained to admit that the other institutions, similar to the Hindu College of Calcutta, planted in various central stations throughout India, will, *in the course of time*, produce *identical* results? I say, "in the course of time," with emphasis, because I would not be the author, or the victim, of Utopian visions. The vast importance of the subject must plead my apology for repeating here, what I have asserted elsewhere, viz., that I do "not anticipate sudden, instantaneous, universal changes. But I do look forward, with confidence, to a *great ultimate revolution* in the social and religious structure of Hindu society,—I do regard the Government enactment, already referred to, as laying the foundation of a train of causes which may, for a while, operate so insensibly as to pass unnoticed by careless or casual observers, but not the less surely, as regards the great and momentous issue. Like the laws which silently, but with resistless power, regulate the movements of the material universe, the present educationary operations, which are of the nature and force of moral laws, will proceed onwards till they terminate in effecting a decisive change in the national mind of India."

But, let it never be forgotten, that, as the Government schemes of education uniformly exclude religious instruction, this may only be a change from a stagnant *superstition* to a rampant *infidelity*.

What then is to be done? Are the Christians of Great Britain to stand idly aloof, and view the onward march of the spirit of innovation in the East, as unconcerned and indifferent spectators. Forbid it, gracious Heaven! What then is to be done? Why, if we are faithful to our trust, and wise *in time*, we may, through the blessing of God, be honoured in converting the education plans of the Indian Government into auxiliaries, that may lend their aid in preparing the way for the spread of the everlasting Gospel!

Wherever a Government Seminary is founded, which shall have the effect of demolishing idolatry and superstition, and thereby clearing away a huge mass of rubbish; *there*, let us be prepared to plant a Christian institution, that shall, through the blessing of Heaven, be the instrument of rearing the beanteous superstructure of Christianity on the ruins of all false philosophy and false religion. Wherever a Government library is established, that shall have the effect of creating an insatiable thirst for knowledge; *there*, let us be forward in establishing our depositories of Bibles and other religious publications, that may saturate the expanding minds of Indian youth, with the life-giving principles of eternal truth.

And who can tell whether, in this way, by "redeeming the time"—by seizing the *present golden opportunity*—we may not be privileged to behold, all the Government schemes of educational improvement in India, overruled by a gracious superintending Providence, for the ultimate introduction of Messiah's reign?

VI. From having formerly said so much on the power of useful knowledge in destroying the systems of Hinduism, it has been strangely concluded by some, that our object has been to reform the natives of India, by means of "knowledge without religion."

Need I say that no conclusion could possibly be more unfounded?

It is, indeed, most true that, for reasons which have more than satisfied many of the wisest and most devoted Christians in this land, I have, with uniform and persevering earnestness, advocated the universal diffusion of sound knowledge in India. Not contented with seeing such knowledge ooze out in scanty drippings, I have toiled and laboured, in conjunction with others, to pour it out in copious streams that may, one day, cover the whole land with the swelling tide of reason and intelligence.

This, however, happens to be only *one-half* of any statement that I have ever, anywhere, made on the subject. And what right has any one, in reason or in justice, to fasten on *one-half* of a statement, and deal with *that half*, as if it were *the whole*?

Strongly and sincerely as I have pled for the diffusion of *sound general knowledge* in India;—have I not, on every occasion, insisted as strongly on the *cotemporaneous* diffusion of *religious truth*? Have I not even laboured to demonstrate that, for the best interests of man in time and eternity, the former should ever be based on the latter—pervaded with the spirit of it throughout—and made to terminate in its exaltation and supremacy? Have I not ever contended for the holy and inseparable alliance of both?—for the reciprocal inter-blending of their different, though not uncongenial, influences? And if one or other must have the precedency, either as respects priority of time or dignity of position, in the mighty work of regenerating a corrupt world;—in the name of all that is reverend and just, let that be selected for the honour, which, by inherent superiority and excellence of nature, is pre-eminently entitled to it.

Without "useful knowledge" man might not live so comfortably *in time*: without "divine knowledge" *eternity* must be lost. How then, could the Missionaries of the Church of Scotland—the Missionaries of a Church, first loosened from Popery by the Wisharts and Hamiltons, subsequently established by the Knoxes and Melvilles, and onwards perpetuated by the Rutherfords and Halyburtons;—how could we dare to sacrifice, at the shrine of a spurious liberality, that highest and sublimest knowledge, whose ennobling truths many of these worthies so heroically died to testify?—Or, if we dared thus to act the part of degenerate children, how could we abide the piercing glance of rebuke which they would cast upon us, if recalled from the realms of day, to witness our treacherous cowardice? And how might we not feel, even now, as if their very ashes would speak out of the tomb, and their blood from under the altar cry out against us!

Such, indeed, and so strong, are my own convictions of the vast importance of useful knowledge in the great work of reforming India, that—were this Venerable House to forbid the diffusion of it in connection with its own Mission—I for one, would feel myself, however reluctantly, constrained at once to relinquish the honourable position which it has been pleased to assign to me. But such, and so overwhelming, are my convictions of the immeasurably superior importance, of that higher knowledge, which unseals the fountain of Immanuel's love, that,—sooner than consent wilfully to withhold it for an hour from the famishing millions of India, or of any other land, in deference to the noxious theories of certain propagandists of the present day,—I would lay down my head upon the block, or commit this body to the flames!

I feel assured, however, that, so far as this House is concerned, it will never fall into either of these extremes. Notwithstanding the charges of religious bigotry that have been so profusely heaped upon it, this House, like its noble reforming ancestry, has been, is now, and, I trust, ever will be, the consistent, the enlightened advocate of all really useful knowledge throughout the wide domain of families, schools, and colleges, whether in this, or in other lands. And, notwithstanding the charges of secular convergency that have been as abundantly levelled at it, this House, like its noble reforming ancestry, has been, is now, and, I trust, ever will be, the intrepid, the unbending advocate of a thorough Bible instruction, as an essential ingredient in all sound education, whether on the banks of the Forth, or on the banks of the Ganges. Yea, may I not be permitted with emphasis to add, that, sooner than consent to surrender this vital principle, which is one of the main pillars in the palladium of the Protestantism of these realms, this House is prepared, as in times of old, to submit to dissolution by the strong arm of violence?—and its members, like their Fathers of the Covenant, prepared once more to betake themselves to the dens and caves of the earth—to wander by the lonely shore or over the desert heath,—to climb the mountain-steep for refuge, or secretly assemble to worship in "some deep dell by rocks o'ercanopied?"

Let it, then, ever be our distinguishing glory to arbitrate between the advocates of untenable extremes. Let us, on the one hand, disown the bigotry of an unwise pietism, by resolving to patronise to the utmost, as in times past, the cause of sound literature and science—lest, by our negligence, in this respect, we help to revive the fatal dogma of the dark ages, that what is philosophically true, may yet be allowed to be theologically false. And let us, on the other hand, denounce the bigotry of infidelity, or religious indifference, by resolving to uphold the paramount importance of the sacred oracles, in the great work of Christianizing and civilizing a guilty world.

Let us, thus hail true literature and true science as our very best auxiliaries—whether in Scotland, or in India, or in any other quarter of the habitable globe. But, in receiving these, as friendly allies, into our sacred territory, let us resolutely determine, that they shall never, never, be allowed to usurp the throne, and wield a tyrant's sceptre over it.

VII. It has been alleged that, in the former statement, there seemed to be something like a denial of what has been well styled by Owen and others, the "self-evidencing power" of the Bible.

If this were the proper time for a theological discussion, I think I might hold myself pledged to prove, to the satisfaction of all reasonable minds, that this is one of the most groundless of charges. I did indeed speak, as I must ever do, not only of the number, but of the *peculiarity* of those difficulties and obstacles that impede the dissemination of divine truth, in a country like India. Many of these are of such a nature, that they admit of being removed by an ordinary application of ordinary means. Are we not, therefore, bound, as creatures endowed with reason and judgment, to employ these means—looking all the while to Heaven for the blessing, which alone can insure success? And how can the prayerful employment of such means be said, in any legitimate sense, to interfere with the self-evidencing power of the Word of God?

Look at the Saviour of mankind at the tomb of Lazarus. Could he not, by one word of his mouth, have caused the great stone to be removed from the mouth of the sepulchre? Beyond all doubt he could. But the removal of the stone was within reach of the power of the assembled multitude. Accordingly, did he not command *them* to remove it? There was that, however, which the assembled multitude could not achieve. Neither their voice, nor the united voice of all the myriads of mankind since the time that Adam fell, could restore life unto him who lay putrifying in the grave. The voice of the Son of God alone could have given efficacy to the command :—"Lazarus, come forth."—By this word of power alone could the iron fetters of the tomb have been burst asunder.

So, in India. If there are any obstacles that seem, in particular cases, to interpose between the souls of men, and the direct application of any of the means of grace ;—ought we not, humbly and prayerfully, to apply ourselves to the removal of these obstacles? And if so, how can our attempting to remove them, be said to impugn the glorious truth, that "the Word of God" is fraught with a self-evidencing power, and is the alone efficacious instrument in awakening and regenerating a guilty and polluted soul?

I rejoice in believing, as in publicly declaring, that "the Word of God" has lost nought of that tremendous power by which it pierceth to "the dividing asunder of soul and spirit, joints and marrow"—nor the sword of the spirit, aught of its keen and etherial temper;—and that, when the Spirit of God powerfully worketh through the instrumentality of "the Word of God," every shred of opposition must be dissipated, even though "principalities and dominions" should league with the powers of earth in the fruitless effort to resist. I rejoice in believing, that, unlike many of the gorgeous, but short-lived, forms of error, divine truth —as revealed in the Bible—is still destined to shine before an astonished world, in its beauty and strength;—that it will scatter to the winds of heaven all the doubts and fears and irresolution of man;—that it will infuse that spirit of divine heroism, which, even in the view of excruciating torments, can resent, with holy scorn, every wretched and cowardly compromise;—that it will finally stalk over the grave of its opponent error—and, if required, in fulfilment of the purposes of an all-wise Providence, once more cause the blood of martyrs to become "the seed of the Church" —and, in its glorious triumphs, run parallel with eternity.

All this, and much more, I rejoice in believing, so far as concerns the capabilities of that Word, which is emphatically termed, "the Sword of the Spirit,"—and the possibilities within the range of a gracious Providence. And yet I see not how all this can abstract one "jot or tittle" from the piety, the wisdom, the propriety on our part, of attempting to imitate the Omniscient God himself, by devoutly endeavouring to adapt all our means, to the accomplishment of all our ends.

VIII. It has been alleged that, in the former statement, there was not a sufficiently explicit reference to the indispensable agency of the Holy Spirit, in the great work of evangelizing a lost world.

My own impression was, and still is, that the distinct recognition of this indispensable agency did pervade the whole of the address, formerly delivered before this Assembly. And had I, for one moment, even suspected that I had not adequately acknowledged what, with my whole heart and soul, I believe,—that is, our entire and unqualified dependence on the influence of the Holy Spirit, for a saving efficacy on all the means of grace—our entire and unqualified dependence on the influence of the Holy Spirit, for the rise, progress, and final consummation of true religion in the soul of man,—I could not have given sleep to my eyes, nor slumber to my eyelids, till I had silenced the upbraidings of conscience by the freest, fullest, and most unreserved acknowledgments, which language would enable me to express. And now, if I only knew how to represent the strength of my own convictions on this most vital subject, in terms proportionally strong, or in terms less liable to misapprehension than those previously employed, most cheerfully would I do it. I believe, that there is a spiritual deadness in the soul, which will yield to no power, save the life-giving energy of the Spirit of God. I believe, that there is a depth of depravity in the soul, which can never be removed, except by the sanctifying influence of the Holy Spirit. I believe, that there is a thick darkness in the soul, which no mere human expedient can ever dispel—and that the omnipotence of the Divine Spirit alone, can enkindle it with the splendours of heavenly light.

IX. It has been alleged that disparagement was formerly cast on "the preaching of the Gospel" to the natives of India.

So far is this allegation from being well-founded, that I ask any man, whether friend or foe, *carefully* to peruse the former statement, and then say, whether it be not in *positive contradiction* to many of its most explicit passages.*

But, if the charge of disparaging the divine ordinance of "preaching" in itself, be not only untenable, but preposterously unfounded—it is still objected that I appear to have "poured contempt" on the preaching of Europeans to the natives of India, through the medium of their own language.

* See second edition, p. 26–28, where there is an elaborate attempt to prove *the necessity of rendering the administration of the ordinance of "preaching" more adequate, efficient, and perfect, than it has ever yet been in India*—as well as *the necessity of multiplying the number of "duly qualified preachers" a hundred, or even a thousand-fold.*"

Nothing that has ever issued from my lips, on this subject, can be fairly alleged to merit the strong appellation of "pouring contempt." If, indeed, the adduction of evidence from the analogy of past history, and the known capabilities of the human mind and its external organs, to prove, what most reflecting persons would be disposed to reckon a *mere truism*, viz., the *comparative* superiority of natives over foreigners, *both being alike qualified, in respect to natural and spiritual endowments*, when addressing *their own countrymen in their own language*;—if this be designated, however unjustly, the "pouring of contempt" on the foreigner's exhibition as compared with that of the *duly qualified* native,—I cannot help it. This is merely the statement of a plain historical fact. And the general fact being an uncontrovertible one, I must,—for the sake of truth, for the sake of India, for the sake of a benighted world,—persevere, in openly and fearlessly proclaiming it. And, if the whole "head and front of my offending" in this matter has been, that I have *plainly spoken out* what the consciences and experience of hundreds must pronounce to be true, whether they openly avow it or not;—may I not, for the sake of advancing the real prosperity of missions throughout the world, be permitted to rejoice in the liberty of speech that has been given me?—Cheerfully willing, to bear my own full share of the disgrace, if disgrace it really be, of not pretending to rival, far less outrival the learned natives of India, or of any other land, either in a *perfect* knowledge of *all* the peculiarities of idiom, or a *perfect* enunciation of *all* the peculiarities of sound, which may characterize their varied dialects and languages! —Cheerfully willing, to submit to the discredit, if discredit it really be, of not pretending to rival, far less out-rival, the natives of India, or of any other country, in the physical capability of withstanding the influence of climate, or in a *perfect* acquaintance with *all* the manners, customs, feelings, sentiments, habits of thought, and prejudices that may distinguish its varied tribes and families!

And here, I must protest against the validity of one very common mode of impeaching the accuracy of the *general rule*, as at present announced. It is based on one of the grossest of fallacies,—even that which converts a *splendid exception from* a general rule, into a *splendid example of* a general rule. To illustrate what I mean.—That females are *not equal* to men in military courage, is surely the *general rule*. Now, how can this be said to be disproved, by pointing to such a dazzling example as that of the celebrated Maid of Orleans, whose feats of heroism outshone, in brilliancy, the entire martial prowess of France? So, in like manner, if the *general rule* be, as I have represented it, that foreigners are not on a level with duly qualified natives, in the style, manner, and effect of their address,—how can this rule be said to be invalidated, by quoting one or more examples from past or present times, in which a learned foreigner may have rivalled, or even out-rivalled, a learned native?

Moreover, if this be the general rule, as to the subject now under review, may I not ask:—Is it wise to make it the general rule to fight against it? Rather, is it not the dictate of wisdom, is it not the demand of duty, so to adjust our plans as to have the general rule on our side?—ready to rejoice, at the same time, at the appearance of any splendid exception, which an overruling Providence may cause to be manifested, for the benefit of any tribe, or people, or nation?

And what is this but, in other words, to describe one grand leading department in the great Missionary enterprise of this Church? Believing the field to be "the world," we have gone forth on a voyage of mercy and benevolence,—and shall not reckon our task accomplished till we have circumnavigated the globe. For reasons, potent and manifold, we made the metropolis of British India, the *first* point of disembarkation. Do you, then, wish to see the millions of India, awakened, regenerated, saved? And is it worse than chimerical to attempt to reach and reclaim *all* of these millions, by the *direct immediate* exertions of a mere handful of foreign agents,—labouring under countless disadvantages? Well, to meet the fearful exigency, and, as speedily as possible, consummate the glorious end, have we not resolved, in humble dependence on divine grace, to rear up "a school of prophets," or religious teachers, who shall diffuse the light and life of Christian knowledge, throughout the length and breadth of the land? And rest we never shall, till, through the divine blessing, we behold arising, a band of native labourers, who, mightily endowed with the acquisitions of sound knowledge, and, above all, with the gifts and graces of the Holy Spirit, shall become *preachers* of the everlasting Gospel to the perishing millions of their own countrymen,—thespiritual Reformers,—

aye, and I will add,—the Luthers, and the Calvins, and the Knoxes of Hindustan! *

X. It has sometimes been impatiently asked,—What, after all, have you done towards the attainment of the proposed objects?—And the question is usually followed up, by a significant reference to the alleged meagreness of the Committee's reports.

I do not appear here, this day, as the advocate of the Committee. Should the occasion require it, they are far more able to defend their own proceedings, than I am. But I do feel it to be incumbent on me this day, in the spontaneous and independent exercise of my own judgment, publicly to declare, that the expectations of many amongst us are worse than unreasonable.

These, first of all, look at the numerous monthly and quarterly papers, and voluminous annual reports of the great Societies in England. And then, turning round, they ask with an air of affected surprise, Why does not your Committee furnish similar papers and reports?—Why!—just *because you withhold the means of enabling them to do so.*

* Let it not be supposed that I look for the *immediate* appearance of *such* a race of men in India. No. But I do look for their appearance *ultimately*. And in order to prepare and hasten the state of things that shall *nurse and rear* such men, I would now, the more diligently, employ all those quickening means which God, in times past, has been pleased to bless. God, in mercy to India, *may* raise up such men sooner than the most sanguine amongst us can anticipate. But, judging from the experience of past ages, I should not hesitate to say, that such men can scarcely be expected to arise during the present, perhaps not even during the next, generation. There *must be a beginning now*. Young men, instructed and trained in our Christian Institutions, will, of necessity, shoot very far a-head of their predecessors.—But the children of these educated natives will possess such prodigious advantages over their fathers, that they, in their turn, may rise to still greater eminence,—both in stability of character and reach of attainments. For it must be borne in mind, that there is an *education of habit* acquired, from constant intercourse in an advanced state of society, which *no mere communication of knowledge* can ever bestow. *For the present*, therefore, from the *infantile* state of improvement in India, the judgment, and energy, and mature experience of enlightened Europeans are indispensably necessary for superintendence and control,—and this necessity may continue for one or more generations yet to come.' But, are we, on this account, to conclude that the necessity must continue for ever? *Because*, in times past, the natives of India, owing to the multiform disadvantages under which they laboured, have been ineffective, without the watchful guidance of Europeans; are we, *therefore*, to conclude that they must continue to be so, in all time coming? *Because*, owing to these disadvantages, they have been enabled to achieve little or nothing, *except in the leading strings* of Europeans; are we, *therefore*, to conclude that they must abide in a state of pupilage and imbecility for ever? No. Such a conclusion were not only unwarranted, but in direct contrariety to many of the lessons of past history. We may rest assured that the very same means, which have raised the descendants of the ancient Britons into such pre-eminence above their savage ancestors, will, if vigorously applied, ultimately raise the sons of India into corresponding pre-eminence above their fathers. Ours, then, be the task,—the noble task,—of beginning now, and putting into operation those means that shall ultimately uplift the natives of India, to the stature of perfect men, in social, intellectual, and spiritual attainments! Then will they be independent of the marshalling skill of Europeans.

Think of the doings of the respected body of Wesleyan Methodists. In numbers, fewer; in wealth, vastly inferior to the Church of Scotland;—how much, think you, do they contribute annually to the cause of their foreign missions?—Upwards of £70,000!—While the Church of Scotland seems to reckon it a mighty matter to contribute £5000! In the City of Edinburgh, the Wesleyan body is almost unnoticed and unknown,—and yet, they raise upwards of £500 for sending the light of the Gospel to heathen lands!—a sum nearly equal to that raised by the National Church of Scotland, in its own metropolis, for the support of its own mission to the regions of pagan darkness!

Notwithstanding all our recent improvement on the score of liberality, as compared with former years, I would ask, in the presence of the assembled representatives of this National Church, whether such a statement is not enough to put us all to shame?—and whether it is not true, that, far from having unsealed, we have not as yet disturbed the very margin of the fountain-heads of Christian benevolence in this land?*

And if the people of Scotland withhold the means, how can they reasonably expect to hear of extensive labours and mighty results? The Church of England, and Wesleyan, and London, and Baptist Missionary Societies, with their princely revenues, are able to establish numerous stations in almost all parts of the world, and maintain hundreds of Missionaries. The bare enumeration of all their stations, and missionaries, and churches, and schools, would form a document of considerable bulk. I put it, then, to the common sense of all present, whether it be reasonable to expect our Committee, with their limited means, and handful of labourers, to rival these great societies in the voluminousness of their reports?—and whether such expectation be not akin to the exaction of the tyranny that commanded "brick to be made without straw?" Only supply your Committee with the necessary means, and, through God's bless-

* Let not this conclusion be evaded by referring to the efforts lately made in the cause of "Church Extension" in Scotland. These have been great, when compared with the *total negligence* of former years:—but the necessities of the case demand that they should be greater still! Have not the Methodists had their cause of Church Extension too? Have they not had to build *all* their own Churches, maintain *all* their own ministers, establish and support *all* their own schools? And yet, *in addition* to all this *at home*—the aggregate of which vastly surpasses what the people of Scotland have ever yet done in the cause of Church and School Extension—the Methodists contribute upwards of £70,000 annually for the propagation of the Gospel *abroad!*

ing, they will be enabled amply to repay you with a redundancy of reports, abounding with the richest variety of interesting details.

I cannot, therefore, allow the notion to be entertained for a single moment, that the Reports of your Committee, *so far as the bare statement of facts is concerned*, do not keep pace with the efforts of your benevolence. Your Missionaries in India, fearful, perhaps to excess, of raising expectations that may never be realised, often suppress many a narrative, glowing with promise, but stopping short of the announcement of actual fruit. And, even in their report of the appearance of actual fruit, they have never been disposed to make the most of the results announced. Facts, the most important, illustrative of the operation of great principles, are often put forth in naked brevity. Facts, which might furnish the text of many a lecture, are often embodied in as many words or short sentences, as, in the hands of some, would call forth the lengthened commentary of whole pages.

Besides, in order rightly to estimate what has been done, people ought to be able to estimate aright the vast disproportion between the agency employed, and the almost overwhelming difficulties to be at first surmounted. But who that has not been in India—or, who that has been there, but has not travailed in pain for the regeneration of her children—can form an adequate estimate of the nature and number of those antagonist prejudices and superstitions which, in durability and magnitude, seem to rival the munitions of rocks?

To confront this terrible array in the midst of hostile millions, what was the opposing agency employed? For nearly two years the National Church of Scotland equipped and maintained in the field only *one* labourer! What a spectacle in the eye of the Christian world! Can imagination itself conceive a situation more pitiable and seemingly more helpless? Is it not enough to remind one of Hall's celebrated remark respecting the lonely willow tree, that reared its drooping head, in the midst of a naked desolated common?—That it looked like nature hanging out a signal of distress!

Think of a whole National Church sending forth, to the distance of ten thousand miles, *one* raw and inexperienced labourer, to stand solitary and alone amid the boundless arid wastes of heathenism!—and say, if it did not look more like the Church hanging out a signal of distress, than bravely unfurling her banners for the spiritual conquest of the nations!

At length an additional fellow-labourer did arrive. And though a third has since followed; and ere long a fourth is to leave the British shores;—still, in point of fact, the *original* ground at Calcutta, has *never* yet been occupied by more than *two at one time!*

Now, when we compare the fruits already reaped by your first Missionaries, with those at first reaped by others in the very same field—instead of lamenting that more has not been done, the throne of grace ought to be approached by all our churches, with the voice of praise and thanksgiving to the Father of Spirits, for the favour and countenance vouchsafed towards his feeble unworthy servants.

On the authority of Mr Townley, one of the first and ablest of the Missionaries of the London Society, I assert that, in the province of Bengal, the first agents of three great Societies—the Church of England, the London, and the Baptist—laboured in pain and weariness for *seven long years,* ere they were privileged to admit a *single* convert into the bosom of the Christian Church! But, long before the expiry of *half* that period, through God's blessing on the labours of your Missionaries, several educated natives of respectable families, and *one* of them a Brahman of the highest caste, were led to bend the knee at the name of Jesus—to adopt the badge of discipleship at the sacred font of baptism—to sit down with British Christians, in sweet fellowship at a communion-table, and there partake of the emblems of the Lord's broken body and shed blood.

And what though, from peculiar circumstances over which we had no control, one and another of those, who received the first impulse towards Christianity from your Missionaries, may have been admitted into the communion of a branch of the Christian Church different from our own,—shall we not rejoice, if they have been rescued as brands from the burning, and their names written in the Lamb's book of life, even though they should be unregistered in the Missionary Records of this church? Yes, verily, we have rejoiced, and shall still rejoice, with exceeding great joy. And, in the name of this Venerable House, let me disown and denounce the worse than anti-Christian bigotry, that would rather not see immortal souls saved at all, than not see them saved as the proselytes of a sect.

At the time your mission was established at Calcutta, the minds of numbers of the most promising of the educated natives, from the operation of the Government system of education without religion, were either turned, or rapidly turning, into the channels of infidelity. Was it nothing to have succeeded, through God's blessing, in arresting a torrent that threatened ultimately to inundate the land with the horrors of irreligious anarchy?—Nothing, to have rendered the very name of Atheism a term of loathing and reproach, instead of being, as it was, the rallying watchword of a wild and reckless liberalism?—Nothing, to have aroused hundreds to read, search, meditate, and inquire into the evidences and doctrines of the Christian faith?—Nothing, to have infused a wholesome leaven into the corrupt mass that has been fermenting ever since, and will go on spreading till India become the Lord's?—Nothing, to have been instrumental, through God's blessing, in leading some of the very ringleaders in this nascent conspiracy against the Lord and his Anointed, to fall down as humble penitents at the foot of the cross?

Was all this nothing? And yet not a tithe of the details connected with these happy results can ever appear in the reports of your Committee.

Again, was it nothing to have succeeded, through the divine blessing, in establishing, within so very limited a period, a large Christian institution,—which, for the number and respectability of its pupils, the efficiency of their intellectual discipline and moral training, and the nature and extent of their combined acquirements, literary, scientific, and theological, has been pronounced by impartial judges to be without a rival, from the lofty Himalaya to Cape Comorin?—An institution, which the highest and most competent authority in the land, the Governor-General of British India, *publicly* declared to have produced "unparalleled results!"

Besides its direct and immediate results in destroying, in the minds of hundreds, the combined powers of ignorance and prejudice, idolatry and superstition, and substituting the ennobling principles of true literature, science, and Christian theology instead—look at the number of problems, fraught with the most momentous bearings on the future destinies of India, which it has helped triumphantly to solve!

Was it nothing, for example, by means of the unrivalled

success with which God had been pleased to crown it, to have demolished the bugbear of alleged impracticability, as regards the attendance of respectable natives, for a series of years, on a Christian Institution—and to have confounded the sophistical reasonings of hollow expediency, on the score of non-interference with the religious prejudices of the natives?—Nothing, to have paralysed the arm of opposition—to have satisfied scepticism itself—and to have converted the suspicions of craven cowardice into unbounded confidence?—Nothing, to have given a higher tone to the sentiments of many of the most influential British residents, on the essential constituents of sound education—to have infused a new and better spirit into some of the older systems—to have generated the desire of remodelling some that were beginning to become effete?—Nothing, to have given such an accelerative impetus to the cause of native instruction, that scores of seminaries have already been established, that otherwise would never have seen the light of day*—and finally, to have provided many of these new seminaries, with duly qualified native teachers, that have received an intellectual, moral, and religious *training* in your central Institution?

And if, as a learned gentleman opposite,† and zealous friend of every Christian enterprise, lately remarked, with admirable point and truth:—If "the schoolmaster be the school:"—in other words, if the minds of the pupils, faithfully reflecting their master's image, must ever be cast in the form and mould of his opinions:—Who can estimate—who can sufficiently magnify the amount of wholesome influence which the Assembly's Missionary Institution, viewed as a grand Normal Seminary for the training of teachers, is likely to exert on the future destinies of India?

Last of all,—Was it nothing, in the metropolis of such an

* "How *numerous*," remarks Mr Trevelyan, in an address to the friends of Education in India, on the influence of example, "how *numerous* are the instances in which visitors to the General Assembly's celebrated Academy have caught the spirit of the plan, and been induced, on their return to their respective districts, to form the nucleus of similar institutions!"

Besides these, there are now, as recorded in the Committee's Reports, several Branch-Schools in immediate connection with the Central Institution, Calcutta. The largest and most advanced of these is the Seminary at Taki, about fifty miles E. of Calcutta: The distinguishing circumstance connected with this seminary is, that it is supported *chiefly* by the *Zemindars* of the place—who contribute between *two and three hundred pounds annually* towards its maintenance.—May not the enlightened liberality of these Hindu proprietors, Kalinath Roy Chaudri, and Baykontonath Roy Chaudri—put to shame many a Christian proprietor in this land?

† Mr Colquhoun of Kellermont.

empire as that of British India, in consequence of the peaceable fruits of righteousness which your institution has produced, to have succeeded in convincing certain timid alarmists in high places, that, as Christianity has never taught rulers to oppress, so will it never teach subjects to rebel?—And to have given a *visibility* of demonstration to the aphorism of the ancient apologist, that then only is a government most sure that it exceeds in friends, when it most surely knows that it exceeds in Christians?

In the name of reason and common sense, I ask, Was all this nothing, as regards the ultimate regeneration of the people of India? And yet not a tithe of the details connected with these happy results can ever appear in the reports of your Committee.

What shall I say more?—for time would fail me, were I to attempt even to allude to all the topics, included in this comprehensive theme. The very noblest department of all,—viz., that of training a duly qualified body of native labourers, who, as preachers of the everlasting Gospel, shall one day cause its glad sound to be heard among the millions of their benighted countrymen,—I pass by unnoticed, because, though rapidly approaching maturity, it is one which, from the very nature of the case, could not hitherto have been brought into actual operation.

Altogether, our missionary undertaking is, as yet, only in its embryo state. It is the unexpanded germ of a mighty system of emanative influence, the full development of which, in all its out-shootings and wide-spreadings throughout the land, the living race of men may never witness. But, through God's blessing, it shall live,—it shall live, and aye be flourishing; and thus tell posterity not merely of the benevolence, but of the suitableness, of the original design,—a design, which simply consists in transporting to the plains of Hindustan, and vigorously applying for its reformation, that very system of "teaching and preaching" combined, which, in the hands of our own Knoxes and Melvilles, once rendered Scotland an intellectual, moral, and religious garden, among the nations of the earth.

Seeing, then, that there are so many efficacious vivifying agencies already at work, and so many more to be soon brought into action—of whose direct and immediate effects we can furnish no statement—though they shall not, on that account, the less surely tell on the generations that are to follow,—I earnestly deprecate all over-sanguine expectations of ***immediate great*** results. Ought we not, on this head, to take warning from the lessons of a past experience? Had the glowing anticipations of many of the original founders of missions been realised, would we, at this day, have been everywhere surrounded by a wilderness of heathenism, almost as impenetrable as ever? No: we should now have been called on simply to gather in the gleanings, after a general vintage of conversion throughout the world. That we may not, therefore, be plentifully sowing the wind of confounded expectations, only afterwards plentifully to reap the whirlwind of disappointment, I crave for patience, I crave for time.

It is not the mere practicability of present plans, but the possibility and desireableness of future achievements, that we regard as the guiding pole-star of our exertions. We desire to benefit, not the *existing* generation alone, but all the generations of a coming posterity. Scorning the pomp and glitter of romantic incident, and ephemeral applause, we labour to lay the foundations of a combined system of intellectual and religious culture, so deep and broad, that it shall advance into futurity, with an annually augmenting increment of force, till the final consummation of all things.

Our object, therefore, is not local or partial, individual or temporary. It is vast and all-comprehensive. It is nothing less than intellectually and spiritually to reform the universal mind of India:—And not merely so, but to embody the essential spirit of the reformation in improved Institutions, that shall perpetuate its blessings to latest ages.

But, has it ever been heard of, that a great and permanent reformation, in any land, has been the work of a day, or a year, or even a single age?—Never, never. A great reformation is not merely the pregnant cause of innumerable happy effects:—It is itself but the aggregate effect of innumerable *predisposing* causes, that may have been accumulating for centuries, ere they became ripe for explosion. Viewed in this respect, the Reformation of Luther has been well compared to the rapids of a river, in its precipitous passage from some mountain range, to the level plains below.

Now, for India we not only contemplate a religious reformation, as effective as that of Luther in Europe, but a reformation still more pervasive, and more thoroughly national.

As yet, however, we are only defiling among the wild,

upland, and mountain ranges of Hinduism,—with its bleak wastes of fable—its arid knolls of prejudice—its frowning crags of superstition—its towering eminences of idolatry. But, already, blessed be God, after the long dark night of forty centuries, has the Sun of Righteousness begun to gild the Eastern horizon. Already, are his earliest beams seen reflected from the frozen summits. Already, are there droppings of truth on many a rocky heart. Already, are there under-currents of inquiry, that shall one day emerge, from the hidden recesses of individual minds. Already, are there evangelical founts, that send forth their little rills of saving knowledge. Already, are the clouds fast gathering, surcharged with the waters of salvation, and ready to pour down their copious showers. And soon may the swollen brooks unite into rivers, and rivers into a mighty stream of quickening influences. For some years more, the mighty stream itself may continue to flow on, through comparatively barren and unanimated solitudes. At length, impatient of restraint, it must burst its accustomed boundaries—and, dashing headlong, in the foam and thunder of a CATARACT OF REFORMATION,—it will gently glide into the peaceful under-vale of time. There, it shall roll on in its majestic course,—overspreading its banks with the verdure of righteousness,—and pouring the fertility of paradise into its pastures of gospel grace,—till it finally disappear, and is lost, in the shoreless ocean of eternity!

Persuaded, as I feel, that such is our present position among the incipient processes that shall, in due time, unite and issue in so glorious a consummation, I, for one, am cheerfully willing to toil on, for years, in feeding, if it be but one, of the little rills of awakening influence,—though I should never live to behold their confluence into the mighty stream of sequences, with its rushing cataract, and waving harvest, gladdening its after-course. And, as regards the ultimate realization of the magnificent prospect, I would, even on a dying pillow, from a whole generation of doubters, confidently APPEAL TO POSTERITY.

XI. Once more I would crave the kind indulgence of this House, while I proceed briefly to notice one other objection urged not against any statement of mine, but against the scheme of Missions generally. It is an objection than which none more insidious or plausible has ever been advanced, and than which none operates more widely or fatally in the communications of private intercourse. Entitled, for this reason alone, to at least a cursory notice, it is doubly so at the present time, on account of its having been lately ushered into notoriety with considerable pomp and circumstance, by one of our great organs of public opinion. The writer, though at a distance, cannot contemplate, without emotion, the great destitution of the means of grace in this northern division of the island. It would seem as if, in the full glow of philanthropic zeal, he could shed tears of commiseration over the spiritual ignorance and heathenism of our neglected and outcast population. And he thus, *in substance*, at once appeals to our piety and our patriotism:—" How can ye, the members of the Church of Scotland, think of sending either men or money to Hindustan, to convert the heathen there, that are aliens in blood, language, and religion;—when ye have so many practical heathens, related to you by ties of kindred and of language, at home, at your very door? And how, by so doing, can ye forget the admonitory exhortation of the holy Apostle, 'He that provideth not for his own, hath denied the faith, and is worse than an infidel?'"

First of all, I might retort on this class of objectors, on the score of their own gross inconsistencies. But waiving, for the present, the subject of inconsistency altogether, and cheerfully conceding the lawfulness of applying analogically the Apostle's aphorism, respecting the supply of temporal necessities, to parallel cases of spiritual destitution, I here take my stand, and declare, that, as employed by the objector, it is at once misquoted and misapplied. And why? For the best of all reasons, that it has been quoted and applied for the express purpose of substantiating an egregiously unsound and unscriptural position.

The position, in few words, is this: "That so long as we have 'practical heathens' or unbelievers at home, we ought not to send either men or money to convert the heathen abroad;" —and, in support of this position, the aphorism of the Apostle is quoted and applied.

1*st*, Now, this position I denounce, in the *first* place, as unsound and unscriptural, because it is in direct opposition to the whole proceedings and example of the holy Apostle himself, during a life of labour, to which nothing similar or second is recorded in the biographies of all ages.

The Apostle himself, we know, gloried in proclaiming the unsearchable riches of Christ, not only to the Jews, but also to the Gentiles, who were "aliens from the commonwealth of Israel, and strangers to the covenants of promise." Yea, and in so doing, he often seemed to glory, if possible, still more than in preaching to his own countrymen, whose were the fathers, and of whom as concerning the flesh, Christ came, who is "God over all blessed for ever." Figure then to yourselves, the inspired Apostle, standing amid the barren wilds of Scythia, addressing a group of fierce roving barbarians, persuading them by the terrors of the law, and the ardours of that love which many waters could not quench, nor the floods of great waters drown, to repent of their sins, and arise and return to that heavenly Father, who, though he winked at the times of their past ignorance, now wills all men to be saved, and come to a knowledge of the truth; and is ready to welcome every returning penitent as a child, and order him to be clothed with the spotless robes of the Redeemer's righteousness. All eyes are rivetted, all hearts arrested. Some are filled with alarm by the upbraidings of an awakened conscience, and the anticipations of a coming judgment; and others are melted into tenderness at the yearnings of Divine compassion that stream from Calvary's cross.

But, hark! suddenly a voice, in the name of Philanthropy, breaks in upon the moving scene. It is directed to the holy Apostle:—"Why, oh! why, have you come hither? Are there not thousands, and tens of thousands of the seed of Abraham—your own kinsmen according to the flesh, who, as yet, refuse to embrace Jesus of Nazareth as their long expected Messiah, and who, by so refusing, fill up the measure of impending vengeance. Why, then, oh! why have you thus forsaken your own unbelieving brethren in Judea and Jerusalem, and come hither to the uttermost ends of the earth, to seek out and convert these rude barbarians, who are aliens in blood, language, and religion?" "Avaunt!"—replies the holy Apostle, with a vehement earnestness of truth, which, like the touch of Ithuriel's spear, unmasks the reptile that daringly assumed the goodly form of Philanthropy—"Avaunt! I know thy voice. Is Christ the Saviour of the Jews only? Is he not also of the Gentiles? Yes, of the Gentiles also. I, therefore, as the disciple of the Lord Jesus, feel myself to be debtor both to the Greeks and to the Barbarians—to the wise and the unwise. And in this I supremely glory, that in Christ Jesus, the Saviour of the world, there is neither Jew nor Greek, Barbarian, Scythian, bond nor free, male nor female. In Him all are one, and there is no difference."

2*d*, In the *second* place, I might proceed at large to show, that the objector's position is grossly unsound and unscriptural, because it is in *direct contradiction* to the parting *command* of our Lord and Saviour—in direct contradiction to the *entire spirit and design of the Christian economy.*

This being the case, I would, with all the emphasis of an overwhelming conviction, assert and maintain, that it is our duty, as a constituted Church of Christ, to do more, tenfold more, than we have ever yet done, towards sending the glad tidings of salvation, *not only* to India, but, as speedily as possible, to *all* the unenlightened nations of the earth. And this I would assert and maintain, for the special reason, among others, that, by *such* faithful compliance with the divine command, and *such* harmonious concurrence with the spirit of Christianity, we might draw down a *larger* measure of the divine blessing on our own heads—and thus be the *better enabled, more effectually to provide for the spiritual necessities of "our own" people at home*—as well as arrest the execution of the divine decree that may speedily come forth, to remove our candlestick altogether, on account of a too long neglected and unfaithful stewardship.

Consider Christianity in its essential spirit. Is it not, like the principle of life, communicative?—and, like the principle of light, diffusive? If, then, we attempt to do violence to this—its essential spirit—by resolving that, so far as we are concerned, it shall not be communicated as spiritual life, nor diffused as spiritual light, among the benighted and famishing nations,—how can we expect the fulness of the divine blessing, even on those labours that are exclusively designed to promote its benign influence, within our own narrow sphere at home?

Again, consider the Saviour's parting command, "Go ye into all the world, and preach the Gospel to every creature." Is it not unambiguous in its language, and peremptory in its authority? Taken in immediate connection with the annexed promise, "Lo, I am with you always, even to the end of the world,"—is it not clear as day, that there is not a command in the Decalogue more absolutely obligatory on the world at large, than this is on the Christian Church? If, therefore, any Church of Christ should presume to neglect or despise this solemn injunction of its Divine Head and Redeemer, how can it expect the fulness of his blessing, even in carrying on the great work of reclaiming sinners and edifying saints within its own circumscribed boundary at home?

Every Christian Church has thus a *double* duty to perform,—one, towards *its own people*, properly so called; and another, towards *the world at large*. If, therefore, while any Church labours to fulfil its bounden duty towards the former, it, at the same time, neglects almost, or altogether, the fulfilment of an equally bounden duty towards the latter:—If, while the one is done, the other is left entirely, or in a great measure, undone:—If, while the one half of the debt is cancelled, the other half is left wholly, or in part, undischarged:—How can such a Church, without self-evident delusion, pray to that God, whose appointed ordinance respecting the universal promulgation of his own eternal word, it practically disregards, for continued health and felicity within its own more immediate pale?

The very law or condition of the existence of Christianity in a state of purity and vigour, is that of constant internal increase: and the law or condition of internal increase is that of perpetual circulation and unrestricted communication outward. In a word, the very law or condition of its continued existence and prosperity, whether in the case of individuals, congregations, or national Churches, is that of *increase by means of free distribution.* And you may as well attempt to counteract this law, immutably impressed upon it by its Divine Author, and yet expect to retain it amongst you in its state of pristine excellence, as attempt to suspend the influence of that "stupendous energy" which causes the periodical revolution of all worlds, and yet expect to retain the earth we dwell upon, in its previous condition of harmony and beauty.

Analogies, though they may somewhat aid the conception, do but very imperfectly represent this law. Christianity is, in the Bible, compared to an expanding tree, that is at length to embrace all nations in its all-covering shade:—attempt to lay a violent arrest on the tree in its growth, and it soon droops, withers, and decays. It is compared to a fountain that ever overflows, and is never exhausted:—attempt to lay a violent arrest on the salient waters of the fountain, and these will soon force an opening elsewhere, and leave the original reservoir dry. It is compared to a shining light, that shineth more and more unto the perfect day:—attempt to lay a violent arrest on the portion of light admitted into your dwelling, and in the very act of so doing, it becomes extinguished. Thus has it been, literally and absolutely, with Christianity under all its dispensations, from the beginning of time;—for, in its substance, Christianity is, "as old as the creation." The law of existence, immutably impressed on it by the Almighty, being that of internal increase—and the law of internal increase being that of communicativeness:—the instant you attempt to lay a violent arrest on its free communication outward:—in other words, the instant you attempt to *monopolize* all its blessings, as if exclusively intended for yourselves, instead of regarding them, agreeably to Heaven's grand design, as *a sacred deposit*, committed to your trust, for the benefit of a lost and perishing world;—that instant, it ceases internally to increase,—and the instant it ceases internally to increase, it begins to shrink and shrivel; it "decayeth and waxeth old, and is ready to vanish away."

What an affecting and overpowering motive does this suggest to the making the work of missions, *i. e.*, the divine work of disseminating abroad the blessings of the everlasting Gospel, not a subject of secondary or subordinate interest, but a subject of prime and paramount importance, that ought ever to engross a full share of the best energies of every Christian Church!

3d, In the *third* place, though the aphorism of the Apostle has been quoted, and applied by the objector in support of a false position, that is no reason why we should not proceed to apply it in support of a true one. The objector has plainly admitted, at least his reasoning has no meaning at all without the admission, that Christians, in general, are bound to provide for the spiritual necessities of "their own." For this most important admission, I would thank the objector from the very bottom of my heart, seeing it supplies me with a new and resistless argument in advocating the *special claims of India.*

Whatever may be alleged of other heathen lands; if it can be shown of India, in particular, that it is now "our own," will it not follow, as an inevitable consequence, from the objector's reasoning, that we are specially bound to provide for its spiritual necessities, and that too, under the impending anathema, that if we do not, we thereby "deny the faith, and are worse than infidels." And if that Christian government which, right or wrong, may have made India "our own," should fail in its high duty in this respect; will it not devolve upon us as a Christian people, and more especially as members of a Christian Church, incorporated with that very Government, to come forth and discharge our share of the obligation?

The only question for determination then is—Whether India, in any legitimate sense of the expression, can be really called "our own?"—For, if so, the question of duty in providing for its spiritual necessities is already peremptorily decided by the objector in the affirmative.

Before an audience like the present, it is only necessary to glance at a few leading particulars. I ask then—Is India, or is it not, "our own?" In the language of Cowper—"Is India free? or, do *we* grind her still?"—Ah! never has any country, through such a long succession of ages, been so terribly scourged as India. Dearly has it paid for its diamond and golden mines—its pearly and coral strands. Look at the unparalleled series of Tartar and Mahammadan invasions. Talk of the volcano, with its sulphureous streams; talk of the earthquake, with its train of chaotic ruins; talk of the hurricane, with its desolating ravages;—all the volcanoes, earthquakes, and hurricanes, recorded since the world began, were but partial and merciful visitations compared with the fiery, crashing, whirlwind eruptions of barbaric hordes into the fertile plains of Hindustan! Look at the oft-repeated massacre of hundreds of thousands of unoffending citizens in cold blood! Look at their mangled bodies literally piled into mountains; and their severed sculls into pyramids! Look at the onward march of the savage conquerors. Before them, all is as "the garden of the Lord"—teeming with plenty, smiling with beauty, and exuberant with the varied bounties of a gracious Providence. Behind them, all is as a desert, naked and leafless, peeled and stripped bare—one vast and profound solitude, where, erewhile, was crowded all that is beauteous in form and pleasant to the sight—one wide and universal sepulchre, where, erewhile, resounded the hum and the bustle of busy men—and the wailings of widowed mothers and fatherless children, where, erewhile, the voices and the notes of happy myriads rolled along in sportive echoings!

Ah! blessed be God, from such terrific desolations India is now at length happily delivered. By a long train of vicissitudes, unexampled in the annals of time, a small island of the ocean, at the distance of a hemisphere,—an island, whose inhabitants were but naked, prowling savages, at a time when India was the very cradle of civilization, legislation, and philosophy, has now succeeded to the imperial sway of a dominion more extensive and consolidated far, than that of the mighty Akbar, or magnificent Aurengzebe! For, which of India's thrones have we not now cast down? Which of its sceptres have we not broken? Which of its treasuries have we not drained? Which of its territories have we not appropriated? What first breathings of impatience under the restraints of our foreign yoke are we not ready to resent as rebellion? What incipient dispositions to transfer allegiance to the lineal representatives of ancient native monarchs, are we not prepared to quash, and capitally punish as high treason against the Majesty of Britain?

Are we not, then, at once the conquerors and sovereign rulers of India? Is not India, therefore, in a peculiar sense "our own?" Are not its people, in the highest and strongest sense of the expression, "our own" people?—"our own" fellow-subjects—subjects of the crown of Christian Protestant Britain, as much as the natives of the Hebrides, or the Catholics of Ireland? Are we not, therefore, bound by every obligation, human and divine, to provide for the spiritual necessities of India's children—the spiritual necessities of famishing millions, whom, contrary to their own will, we have compelled, by force of arms, to become "our own" adopted children? Yea, are we not doubly bound to impart to them the treasures of useful knowledge and of gospel grace, as the only adequate equivalent in our power, in reparation of the wrongs, grievous and innumerable, which in times past they have sustained at our hands? As far as good intentions are concerned, ours may now be truly characterised as a paternal Government, that seems sincerely desirous to redress every injury and staunch every bleeding wound. But who can obliterate the long black catalogue of treachery and plunder, devastation and death, that swells the revolting narrative of many of our earlier conquests? Ah! there have been deeds perpetrated by the sons of Britain on the plains of Hindustan—deeds, that in number cannot be reckoned up in order—deeds of unutterable infamy—deeds that are engraven in characters of blood in the ineffaceable pages of history,—ay, and registered, as an eternal memorial against us, in the book of God's remembrance! And shall we withold the only adequate boon which it is in our power to confer, by way of recompense, on poor, ransacked, pillaged, ravaged, unhappy India? Ah! if we do, methinks the spirits of thousands, untimely slain, will rise up in judgment to condemn us. Methinks, a long eternity of retributive vengeance will seal the merited condemnation. But let us now, if ye will, resolve to shroud the misdeeds of our fathers in the mantle of oblivion. And, over the plains which they have drenched with the blood of the victims of a mercenary policy—and along the shores which they have strewn with the wrecks of a griping avarice,—let us, their descendants and kinsmen, resolve to rear the temples of Zion;—those precious monuments of piety and benevolence, which, in real glory, outstrip the regal pyramid, and, in the duration of their effects, outlast the fabric of the material universe!

XII. Though much yet remains unsaid of what was originally intended, the failure of time and strength compels me to hasten, however abruptly, to a conclusion.

And, in doing so, bear with me when I give vent to the overpowering emotions of my own heart, by exclaiming in the hearing of this great Assembly:—Oh, that as a Protestant nation, and a Protestant Church, we were made to know, at least in this the day of our merciful visitation, our high and godlike destiny, as the Zion and Jerusalem of these latter times, whence gladsome light and liberty might emanate to the remotest ends of the earth! The men of Athens, Pagans though they were, could, with one simultaneous voice, unite in the patriotic shout —"Let us march against Philip: let us fight for our liberties: let us conquer or die." And is it not high time that we, as a Christian people, should join in raising a far loftier note?—A note, that might be sublimely responded to by prophets, and apostles, and the whole noble army of martyrs that now encompass us around, as intensely interested spectators, bending from their heavenly thrones? And where, oh, tell me, where can this loftier note be first raised more worthily than in this very Assembly—the representative Assembly of a Church founded by a race of heroes, whose dauntless spirit, amid cruel sufferings and death, amply proved that on them the mantle of prophets, and apostles, and martyrs had largely fallen? In order to realise so blessed a consummation, would to God that all petty jealousies and ungodly rivalries were for ever annihilated from amongst us! Would to God that all unholy oppositions of partisanship were for ever banished from our shores!—oppositions about questions, many of which, compared with the conversion of a world of lost sinners towards God, are so contemptibly insignificant, that for a whole nation to be agitated by them into turbulence and fury, does indeed,—

> "Resemble ocean into tempest wrought,
> To waft a feather or to drown a fly!"

Oh, then, that the middle walls of partition, which at present sever the bleeding Churches of Christendom into so many hostile sections, that frown defiance from each others battlements, were riven asunder! Oh, that all that profess the faith of Jesus, of whatever name or denomination among men, were melted down by the lightning of Divine love, and fused into one homogeneous mass, actuated by one spirit, and raising the one universal shout:—Let us march against the common enemy of man: let us fight for the spiritual liberties of a world: in the cause of the Redeemer, let us conquer or die.

Will this be branded as wild enthusiasm by the cold calculating spirits of a boastful intellectual age? With righteous indignation I must repel the charge. Is it lawful for the British patriot's breast to throb when he hears the orator exclaim, amid the deafening plaudits of a senate, "where the standard of England is planted, there, foreign dominion shall not come?" And is it not a higher and holier enthusiasm in the patriot citizen of Zion to exult, when he hears a voice from heaven's canopy proclaim—where the standard of the Cross is planted, there, Satan's dominion shall not come? Is it lawful for the British patriot's heart to vibrate with an undefinable thrill of ecstatic joy, when he listens to the poet's song of the meteor flag of England, which,—

> "Has braved a thousand years
> The battle and the breeze?"

And is it not a higher and holier enthusiasm in the patriot citizen of Zion to exult, when he bears aloft the flag of the everlasting covenant, which, for six thousand years, has withstood more than the shock of a thousand navies, manned by human and hellish foes?—which still shall brave "the battle and the breeze" of conflicting moral elements—which shall survive the funeral obsequies of sin, and death, and the grave,—and finally wave, in triumph, over the citadels of the nations, when all their pomp and grandeur are swallowed up and lost, amid the overpowering glories of Messiah's reign?

With visions so bright spreading out before us, in the prophetic page, shall we not arise and shake off all earthly dalliance and delay? Shall we not arise and put on the whole armour of God?—Ours is no ordinary warfare; ours, no ordinary struggle.—Oh! let us then arise and go forth to the contest, cheered by the songs of divine chivalry, and animated by the certain prospect of the victor's crown. Let us go forth in the spirit of ancient warriors, who fought the good fight, and are now inheriting the promises. Let us go forth in the name of Jehovah, Lord of Hosts. Let his standard be triumphantly planted. Let truth and righteousness, salvation and peace, be emblazoned on all our banners. Then shall we be unconquered, and pronounced unconquerable. And then, through our conquest shall the Church of Scotland be hailed as a blessing by the perishing millions of Hindustan—become a praise and a glory in the whole earth—and cause the chorus of the redeemed swell the louder, when, riding on the chariot of triumph and attired in the royal robes of victory, they enter the mansions of eternal joy!

THE END.